HOW TO
Make Money With Dolls

By Mildred Seeley

HPBooks

Mildred Seeley shown with four dolls, from left to right: AT7, wire-eyed Steiner, Bru Jne 3 and AT2.

ABOUT THE AUTHOR

Mildred Seeley has been involved in doll making and doll collecting for nearly 40 years. She and her husband, Vernon, were the former owners of Seeley's Ceramics. Mildred is a noted authority on doll making, antique doll appraising and doll photography. She also works as a consultant to doll businesses, gives lectures and holds seminars on antique dolls.

Studying art, sculpture and painting has given Mildred a more-comprehensive background to appreciate and participate in doll collecting. She holds a master's degree in art education. Mildred has written four other books for HPBooks—*Doll Collecting for Fun & Profit, Doll Costuming, How to Collect French Bébé Dolls* and *How to Collect French Fashion Dolls.* She has written other books on dolls and doll making and was the founder of the Doll Artisan Guild, an organization of porcelain reproduction-doll makers.

SPECIAL THANKS

I wish to thank my husband, Vernon, for all his help with the business of dolls, and my son, Jay, for his help, especially with the educational material.

Published by HPBooks
A Division of HPBooks, Inc.
P.O. Box 5367
Tucson, AZ 85703
(602) 888-2150
ISBN: 0-89586-302-2
Library of Congress Catalog Card Number: 85-82499

Printed in U.S.A.
1st Printing

Publisher: Rick Bailey
Executive Editor: Randy Summerlin
Editor: Judith Schuler
Art Director: Don Burton
Design and Assembly: Kathleen Koopman
Production Coordinator: Cindy Coatsworth
Typography: Michelle Carter
Director of Manufacturing: Anthony B. Narducci
Cover Photography: Ray Manley Studios, Tucson, AZ
Illustrations: Arlene Dubanevich Seeley

Previous page: French dolls are good investments and have increased in value. Long-Faced Jumeaus, like this one, can be worth a great deal. This one is valued at $12,000. Twelve years ago she could have been purchased for $2,000. A good doll is often better than money in the bank.

Table of Contents

How to Make Money With Dolls

We are fortunate to live during this new "age of dolls"—dolls are one of the best money-making items in the world today. You may feel you deserve a piece of the "doll pie," or you may have a small piece and want to know how to make it bigger. In this age of the doll, you may want to hurry and start a business *now* before you look back and say, "That was the time when millions were being made on the universal toy—the doll—and I missed out on it." No one knows about dolls and the money that can be made with them better than I, who unintentionally started the reproduction-doll movement and found success without ever dreaming it was possible.

The doll movement became a bandwagon for every mold-making company, ceramic company and toy company to jump on. The doll movement has served as a money-making vehicle for magazines, newsletters, price guides, books and directories. There is still room for more people to reap the joys and make money from working with dolls.

Dolls have been with us for a long time, and they probably always will be in some form. Every girl has probably had a doll, and almost every boy has wished for one. Dolls are popular all over the world, and people never outgrow them.

Antique dolls are collectors' items of great worth. New dolls being made today will be antique dolls someday. The field of dolls is growing because dolls are creative, enjoyable things to work with. It's no wonder people love to work with dolls and enjoy making money at the same time.

Financial success in the field of dolls has come, is coming and will come from many directions or combination of directions. Success has come from *writing, selling, creating, reproducing, photographing, auctioneering, repairing, insuring, promoting, publishing and teaching* about dolls.

Left: Mechanical dolls have increased in popularity over the last few years. Mechanized works are available for doll makers to make their own porcelain mechanical dolls. Old mechanicals need people who can repair them. These dolls are a great addition to a collection, but many don't work. This is a marked F.G., and she beats up a storm.

Success in selling dolls has been most obvious in the last 15 years. Fortunes have been made through selling antique dolls in shops, at doll shows, through the mail or over the kitchen table. Another area of success is the doll auction, which is an innovation of the last 15 years.

Some people have become successful making and selling their own reproduction dolls. Some people have sold other people's reproduction dolls. Some original-doll artists make and sell their own dolls, and a few have sold their designs to toy companies and made their money on royalties they receive.

Success in dolls also comes from writing about dolls—antique dolls, their history, their costumes, their construction, their makers and many other interesting aspects. Success has come from writing about reproduction dolls—how to make them, their problems, their costuming, their mold making.

Books and articles have been written about identification of old dolls. Much has been written about the success of doll makers. Some magazines are published solely for doll people. Doll price guides are published each year to keep up with ever-changing prices in the doll world. Directories are available so people can find what they want and who makes it.

Photographing dolls has developed into an art form, and photos of dolls have been used in books, magazines, cards, stickers, calendars, prints and posters. From photos, lithographs have been made to decorate doll plates and other porcelain objects.

Everyone knows there are only a limited number of antique dolls available and more collectors every day, so each doll must be carefully preserved and repaired, if necessary. Doll "hospitals" are swamped with repairs.

New policies have been developed for insuring doll collections. Insurance agents have found a new way to make money by adding a fine-arts rider for dolls to the homeowner's policy or separately insuring the entire doll collection.

A few years ago, public doll shows were unheard of—today, many promoters put on doll shows. People are learning to be promoters and are putting on their own doll shows, conventions and seminars—for money, of course.

Jim Fernando's jolly Jollies shows this doll maker's creative ability. He also dresses dolls in exquisite reproduction costumes. See my Snow Angel, page 126.

Publication of doll books has made many people very successful. Doll-magazine publishing has increased dramatically. Success in publishing has been achieved with magazines, books, price guides, newsletters and directories—all about dolls.

If you want to hear about other success stories, talk to the best instructors of doll classes, seminar teachers or even studio operators.

Dolls have been passage to the land of opportunity for many, many people.

DOLLS AS TANGENTS TO EXISTING COMPANIES

We think of how computers have changed the world, but a small loved object—the doll—has also made its mark. It has changed the world of many people who are happy making a doll by hand. Dolls have also meant a great deal of money to big businesses.

In the last few years, old companies, such as Gorham (originally a silver company), have entered the world of dolls. Gorham has produced an entire line of dolls, with extensive advertising. Royal Dalton, known for its fine china and figurines, has added a line of dolls. Bing and Grondahl added dolls to their figurine line. Recently, America's famous china company, Lenox, produced their first dolls. Lesser-known companies have added doll figurines and dolls to their existing lines.

Limited-edition plate manufacturers now produce some doll plates. I started the first doll-plate series, called *The Doll Collection,* in 1978. New plates are added each year.

Dolls have also become part of large companies, such as Hallmark with their doll cards and calendars. Creative Teaching Press, which makes art materials for schools, now sells stationery, stickers and cards decorated with illustrations of dolls.

Travel agencies have also realized money could be made with dolls, and many now offer tours aimed at people interested in dolls. These are not new travel agencies or tour agencies but ones that have expanded to include tours especially for doll lovers.

Dolls were once sold at auctions, along with antiques and household goods, or at estate sales. Now the world's largest auction houses—Christie's, Sotheby, Butterfield and Butterfield, and others—auction dolls separately. They realized the amount of money that could be made in this area. A new policy, called *absentee bidding,* has been added, and now anyone, anywhere in the world can bid on a doll without having to be at the auction in person. Even phone-in bids on the day of the auction are accepted by some auction houses.

Beckett dolls are each handcarved and unique. See the "Dollionaire" story of the Becketts on page 99.

Probably one of the greatest success stories in the last few years is Theriault Auctions. We attended one of their very early auctions in a tiny auction room in Wavery, Pennsylvania. The Theriaults had a few dolls and some used furniture. When they realized how much money could be made with dolls, they decided to auction dolls full time. Now they hold first-class auctions each month in large cities all over the country. They have a reputation for selling the most expensive antique dolls, and they treat their customers as special guests.

Some companies, like Kemper Tools who made ceramic tools for many years, added a doll-supply department. Duncan Ceramic Supply added doll molds and tools to their line of ceramic supplies.

Existing doll and toy companies have seen the doll in a new light, and they are making dolls for collectors. Horsmann and Effanbee are now making dolls for adult collectors, in addition to children's play dolls. Some companies make reproductions of dolls their company made earlier, such as Baby Dimples, Shirley Temple and Ginny. Some companies make newly created dolls for doll collectors. Other companies reproduce old advertising-dolls, such as the Gerber Baby, the Campbell Kids, the Morton Salt girl and others.

Many of the country's largest promoters of ceramics shows, antique shows and gun shows now hold very successful doll shows. The Anaheim Doll and Miniature Show is held each April in the Anaheim Convention Center by promoter Larry Bohler, who originally ran ceramic shows. The Eastern National Antique Doll and Toy Show is held twice a year in Washington, D.C. It has 600 booths and is one of the largest shows in the country. Bellman Promotions, Inc. sponsors the show; the company originally put on antique shows.

The hobby ceramic industry has turned almost entirely from making household decoration items to hobby doll making. Former ceramic studios have changed their names and the way they operate to accommodate porcelain dolls rather than low-fired ceramics. This meant new kilns that fired porcelain, new doll molds and learning to work with porcelain. Ceramic studios that have not changed to dolls have steadily declined.

Suppliers to ceramic studios also saw the light; they added molds and supplies for doll makers. Many companies became supply companies and now make materials only for dolls. Seeley Ceramic Service of New York (the company, my husband Vernon and I started) began as a ceramic supply house. Today, it is a multimillion dollar business doing over 85% of its business in doll supplies. Other ceramic companies, such as Bell, Byron, and Sams, have changed the focus of their ceramic business to dolls.

A small printing company began printing doll material, then saw the unrealized potential in the doll world, so it became a publisher of doll material in magazine form. The company branched out to doll books. The doll magazine, *Doll Reader,* is published by Hobby House Press, and it demonstrates what dolls can do for a company in a short time. Another example, the magazine *Dolls* published by Collectors Communications Corp., has achieved its stature in only a few years.

Another company, A&R Products, produces material to make mannequins. Mannequins are used in stores, and they are used many times. It was discovered the same material used for mannequins makes a fine "composition" body for doll bodies, similar to the composition used for old doll bodies. Today, mannequin material is used for production dolls and doll bodies for hobbyists. This existing company used dolls to expand their business.

It is obvious many large companies that make money with dolls today were already in existence when they added dolls. They added a department, started a side line or created a tangent company when they saw the potential in dolls.

NEW COMPANIES

New companies, large and small, have come into existence over the past few years. Jan Hagara is one entrepreneur who formed her own company to produce doll figurines (dolls without moving parts), dolls, plates with pictures of dolls and lithographs of dolls.

Some companies, such as Robert Dankanies' The Dollhouse Factory in Lebanon, New Jersey, was formed to make doll houses.

New doll shows and new promoters fill doll magazines with display ads for their shows. One recent issue of the *Doll Reader* had 56 doll shows advertised; many of the "promoters" are new to the field.

Paper dolls were included in early ladies' magazines, but today paper-doll artists produce dolls that are included in many doll magazines. Creators of paper dolls, such as Pat Stahl, Susanna Oroyan, Carol-Lynn Waugh, Peggy Jo Rosamond, Jean Woodcock, Charles Ventura, Emma Terry and the late Ellery Thorp, make lovely paper dolls.

Dolls are being made in Europe for collectors, so we have importers who resell them to dealers. Hobby Enterprises, Inc., of West Caldwell, New Jersey, and F.N.R. International Corp., of Lawrence, Massachusetts, are two companies that import dolls to resell in the United States.

Many original-doll artists have formed their own companies to make beautiful dolls for collectors. One artist, Susan Cathey Dunham, makes and sells dolls in limited-edition productions.

Dollsparts, of Long Island City, New York,

started early in the doll boom. Originally it was a doll-wig company; today it sells many kinds of doll supplies, such as shoes, wigs, books, hats and bodies. Many doll-supply companies have come into existence and have found success in recent years.

Ten years ago it was almost impossible to find a pattern to make a doll costume. Today, many talented people have learned the art of pattern making and are producing usable patterns for old and new dolls. These patterns are sold by the makers or by distributors. Lyn of Lyn's Doll House in Denver, Colorado, sells her own well-made patterns. Hazel Ulseth and Helen Shannon produce bonnet patterns and dress patterns for dolls; they sell directly to customers by mail and through distributors. Brown House Dolls and many other companies also sell patterns through the mail.

Some people make reproduction parts for old dolls, such as replacement hands, feet and shoulderplates. One expert owns Joyce's Doll House of Parts in Mt. Clemens, Michigan. She makes all kinds of doll arms, legs and shoulderplates of porcelain bisque.

Teaching—in doll studios, at seminars and at conventions—has become big business for many excellent teachers, and hundreds of teachers are doing well today. They are financially successful and happy in their chosen profession.

Doll museums have appeared in every state. Many museums are new; others reopened after being closed for years. Some were old, general museums that added on a room or a wing for dolls. Some museums produce newsletters and have members who help the museum financially.

Doll-mold companies, producing molds from antique French and German dolls, have also been successful. Many of these companies also produce doll-body molds and "composition" bodies to go with doll heads. These companies have been successful selling body molds and head molds.

Businesses have been built around small things, such as doll shoes or doll eyes. Some companies make globes and cases for easy display of one doll or many dolls together.

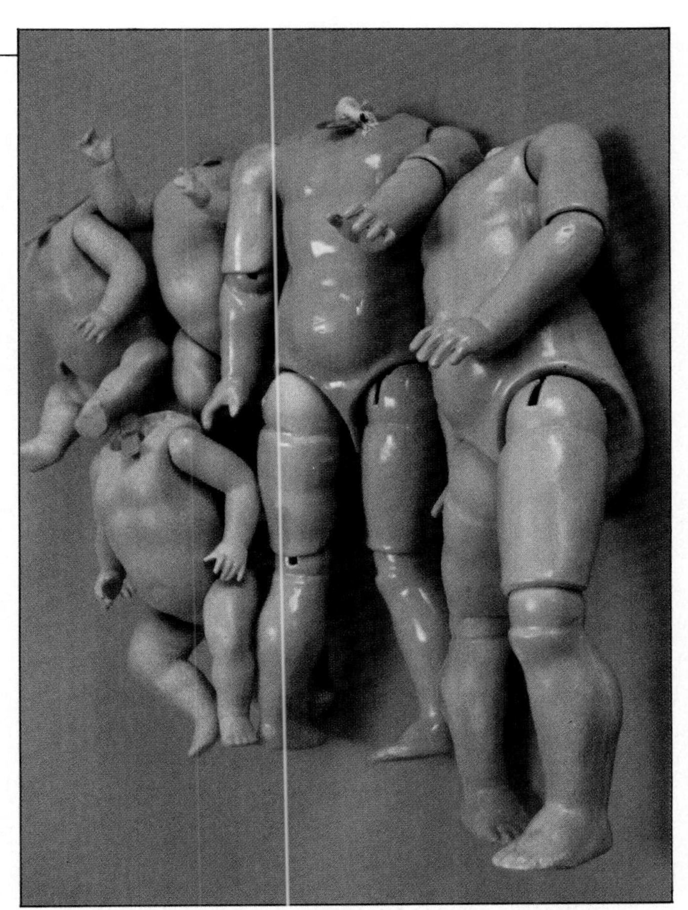

Composition doll bodies are made for reproduction dolls and for replacement of bodies on antique dolls. The doll-body business is a good one.

These are just a few of the successful fields of business in the world of dolls. Anyone with ambition, drive and know-how can make it in the world of dolls.

NEW IDEAS WORK

Kemper Tools recently came up with a novel idea. They sponsored a working, educational cruise for doll makers. The group, using Azure Seas Lines, sailed from Los Angeles to Ensenada, Mexico. The workshop cruise included demonstrations and classes by Connie Derig and Judy Meier. Participants viewed videotapes, such as "Dolls by Dottie" and "Joyce's Doll Repair." There was even a lecture on the business of doll-studio management.

KEMPER TOOLS P.O. Box 696, Chino, CA 91710 (714) 627-6191 Issue 84, Vol. 2

WORKSHOP CRUISE TO MEXICO - JOIN US!

The 1985 Kemper Workshop Cruise has been announced by Herbert H. Stampfl, President of Kemper Tools and Kemper Doll Supplies. This unique fun-and-learning week begins on Sunday, June 2, 1985, and is open to any Kemper customer. Upon arrival at Los Angeles International Airport, you will be greeted by a special representative and chauffeured to your first-night luxury hotel accommodations. That afternoon you may pick from the first two workshops to be offered. In the evening, Mr. Stampfl will host the Presidents Welcome Banquet where fifteen Kemper Suppliers will be honored for their sales increases between November 1, 1984 and April 30, 1985. Five shops will be presented with cash awards of $250 each, five shops will earn $100 each, and the five top sales leaders will earn their entire week for two FREE. The Sales Increase Contest is for Kemper Distributors and Wholesalers only.

Monday will begin with a Continental Breakfast followed by two workshops. All workshops will be presented by top industry Artisans/Experts to enhance your enjoyment. After lunch, everyone will be chauffeured to the Cruise Ship for the

spectacular afternoon departure. The Cruise is complete with fabulous food, live entertainment, movies, parties, gambling casino, games, and finest modern staterooms. Tuesday the ship will dock in San Diego Harbor from 9 am to 4 pm for sightseeing. A choice of two seminars await you from 4:30-6:00 after departure.

Wednesday the ship will dock in Ensenada, Mexico, and you can join us on our special Kemper Shopping/Sightseeing Tour or enjoy the day on your own.

Thursday there will be two special "high seas" seminars on board ship. Friday morning the ship will return to Los Angeles Harbor and you may choose either to use the limo service back to the airport or to continue your stay in Southern California. Special tour packages are available.

Cost of the Kemper Workshop Cruise, hotel, all meals, all workshops, port tax and limo service is only $695 per person plus airfare. Special airfares are available and are tax deductible! Space is limited so your reservations and $100 deposit (per person) must be received by Kemper no later than November 30, 1984. For further information and rules for the Sales Increase Awards, call or write Kemper today. Join us for this fabulous, unprecedented event—you'll be glad you did!

Doll workshops were arranged around the ship's activities, and everyone had a free day in San Diego and Ensenada. One of the organizers, Dianne Anderson from Kemper Tools, reported that the trip was fun, relaxing, educational and a great success. It was a novel idea. See flyer above.

The UFDC (United Federation of Doll Clubs) had its first luxury cruise on the Holland America Line in the spring of 1986. The week-long cruise went to the Caribbean from Ft. Lauderdale. Many different doll activities were offered during the course of the cruise. The cruise visited San Juan, Puerto Rico, St. Thomas, the Virgin Islands and the Bahamas. People who participated said it was a "wonderful educational experience!"

Dolls have also inspired other trips; doll tours have become popular over the last few years. See flyer on opposite page. Some tour

A Doll-lightfull European Fantasy Tour 1984 BILL AND MARTHA MARTIN*

CREATORS OF "WISTFUL DOLLS" INVITE YOU TO PARTICIPATE WITH THEM IN. .

A FUN-FILLED EUROPEAN EXTRAVAGANZA

OCTOBER 2 - 22, 1984

Traveling this playground of princes, you will visit, in-depth, museums, doll shops and factories, such as the Lenci Doll Factory in Turin . . . PLUS THE:

SECOND INTERNATIONAL GLOBAL DOLL SOCIETY CONVENTION, LUCERNE

OCTOBER 4 - 7th

Including workshops, lectures and souvenirs!!!
You will visit such historic countries as:

ITALY — GERMANY
SWITZERLAND
AND SOUTHERN FRANCE

When in Rome, you visit the magnificent Sunday Flea Market, with many chances to purchase regional and antique dolls. But that's not all; fully escorted, first class hotels and most meals included and much more.

LAND TOUR PRICE
$2098; per person double occupancy.

FOR INFORMATION PLEASE CONTACT:
* your tour directors since 1977 . . .

BILL AND MARTHA MARTIN, (ODACA)
924 EDGECLIFF DR., LANGLEY, WA 98260
(206) 321-6335 **OR**
STEPHEN L. RUSH, CTC.
PRESIDENT CROSSROADS TRAVEL
206-746-2202

CROSSROADS TRAVEL inc.
*Suite Q1, Crossroads Mall, Bellevue, Wa. 98008

Left and above: Doll tours and cruises are the newest way to involve doll lovers in the world of dolls. A vacation, such as a tour or cruise, may be considered a business expense.

companies have added doll tours to their regular agendas. Doll conventions in this country often have local doll tours to museums and businesses before and after a convention. Doll conventions in Europe have added tours before and after a convention. Tours of 10 to 14 days duration in Europe visiting doll factories, doll makers and private collections are also becoming popular. Some tours are run by individuals already in the doll business; some are run by entrepreneurs who want to make money.

Doll people consider cruises and tours as something special. They are educational opportunities—plus a vacation—that can be treated in a special way on your tax form.

Consult your tax accountant before you go on a "business vacation" because some tax laws are changing. You're working vacation could be a tax write off.

SPECIAL ACTIVITIES

At the 1985 UFDC Convention, held in Atlanta, someone came up with a very novel idea. At the first dinner meeting, a special club was proposed—*Collect a Friend Club*. This club has no dues or limited membership, and most other rules and regulations of clubs don't apply.

This was a friendship club; all you had to do was introduce yourself to other members wearing the No. 1 button. (People wearing the No. 1 button were first-time convention attendees.) You were asked to get to know these people and put names of three No. 1 button wearers on a slip of paper. If you collected a few more names, you were eligible for an office in the newly forming club. This was a fun activity to make newcomers feel welcome, and it created a friendly atmosphere immediately.

In 1985, the *Doll Reader* came up with the idea of the *DOTY awards* (Doll of the Year). These awards allowed everyone to vote on dolls they liked best. Dolls were displayed at the UFDC convention and shown in the *Doll Reader* magazine. It was different, and many doll lovers participated.

WORLD DOLL DAY

An idea I'd like to mention is *World Doll Day*. You probably haven't even heard of this special day, which is held the second *Saturday* (usually the day before Children's Day) in June. I launched this event in 1986. This is a very special day for doll makers, doll collectors and children because it's the day doll lovers give a doll to a child.

We all remember how much a doll meant to us as children. We also remember it didn't matter how many dolls we had—another was always welcomed.

World Doll Day is a day of great joy to the giver *and* receiver. It makes many people happy. It doesn't matter the age of the child to whom you give a doll because we are *all* someone's child, and we're all children at heart! It doesn't matter about the age or price of a doll; it's the idea that counts.

Mothers and grandmothers can go to a studio and make dolls for the occasion. Doll-shop owners love the idea because dolls are purchased. Other people will take their old dolls out of trunks and pass them on to relatives. Doll clubs have special meetings; some clubs hold doll shows so people can purchase dolls for this special occasion.

World Doll Day is a time for displaying and introducing new dolls; it's a time for doll fairs. It gives advertisers a new gimmick, and it gives writers and magazines a new doll event to cover. It draws the children, our next generation, into the world of doll lovers.

On Mother's Day, a mother gets flowers. On Father's Day, a father gets neckties. But for Children's Day—who gives the children anything? Children's Day is not a national holiday, and many people don't even know about it. With World Doll Day occurring near Children's Day, many children can get a doll for this day. We must not neglect boys and men—they also love dolls.

This day is one of the big events of the doll world. Dolls and the joy of dolls deserve a day, as do all children.

The first World Doll Day was June 14, 1986. I personally gave a doll to a child. There are many children who have no dolls. If you don't know any children, you can plan each year to give a doll to a grownup child in the family or just a friend.

You can ship a doll to another country. I have always felt dolls could be instruments of world understanding. From the time I first started writing books on doll making, I had the hope that dolls would help make friends all over the world and develop love among us all.

World Doll Day is a day for doll exhibits. It is my hope libraries will have special doll displays and museums will publicize their dolls with special exhibits at this time each year.

Above: This is the logo for World Doll Day. Copy this one or contact the printer, Isbell Printing Co., listed on page 124.

Right: Mil Seeley portrait doll created in its entirety by Boots Tyner from a photo of me as a child. Boots no longer does portrait dolls but sells the molds of dolls she makes. Molds of this one are for sale.

BEING SUCCESSFUL WITH DOLLS

With the thousands of "Dollionaires," (people who have become successful through dolls), we often find a combination of things that have contributed to their success. Before I go on, let me define dollionaires—they are people in doll businesses who are financially successful, happy or successful *and* happy.

Many of these people have told me they attribute their success to being able to recognize, to know and to believe in what they can do. Some say it was their willingness to learn, study and improve their own techniques. Some say it was talent. Some say it was their business training. Others believe their success was due to their ability to get along with others and share their knowledge. Read about these successful doll people in the following pages and see what you can apply to your own life to carry you to the top of the doll world.

Some people have written their own stories, and some I interviewed. I found the stories of how they started and how they became successful so intriguing that it was difficult to choose and know which ones you would find most helpful. I have included as many stories as I could squeeze between the covers. There are thousands more out there who should have been mentioned. Dollionaire stories are found throughout the book.

Magazines may put out special editions. Doll stores may hold selling campaigns in the weeks before World Doll Day. Doll makers will make special dolls for the occasion. There will be doll competitions with World Doll Day awards of plaques and trophies.

The logo, shown on page 12, is made from artist Boots Tyner's portrait doll representing me as a child. See page 13. The child carries an antique German bisque doll to represent the doll collector's gift. Feel free to copy the logo or have more made using this illustration.

I need only one thing to make World Doll Day a continued success—your *cooperation*. I need cooperation from doll collectors, doll magazines, doll newsletters, doll shops, libraries, doll makers, mothers, grandmothers, fathers, grandfathers and anyone else involved in the doll world.

This is an event for everyone because there are no fees, permission is not needed, there are no obligations and no one owns the day. I urge all doll lovers to observe the day and its ideas each year.

SEELEY'S MARQUE DOLL

An example of how one doll can work for you is illustrated in the following story. About 10 years ago, I purchased a Marque doll that we named André. In 1983, another Marque doll sold for $38,000 at the Scottsdale (Arizona) Doll Auction. There was no logical way I could explain to myself that buying André was a good investment. I had to account to my conscience in some way.

At that time, there were limited-edition plates. I came up with the idea of a limited-edition *doll*—from the Marque head. I believe this was the first limited-edition doll ever made—now there are hundreds.

My husband, Vernon, carefully made molds of the Marque head, hands and feet. We made a limited number of dolls and dressed each one like the original and sold them for $650 apiece. It was the highest price ever paid for a reproduction doll. After the success of this first limited-edition doll, we made molds of his Marque sister, Alyce, and sold a limited number of her. I used the dolls in four different books on dolls, and I used them a different way in each book. We made a reduced-sized head mold and sold it. I also used both Marque dolls on limited-edition plates that I produced and sold.

This story is an example of how one doll can work in many different ways for you. Dolls don't work by themselves—you must put forth a lot of effort and time to make them produce a profit. I never give a seminar or slide presentation without including my Marque dolls.

When I wrote a book on milettes, I realized a small Marque doll would be well-received. I made a little Marque mold to go with other small French dolls. I have received a royalty from the mold for several years. I also had posters made of the boy Marque in his original costume. We had posters made of several old French dolls at the same time and sold these at doll shows and doll meetings. The Marque is also being used on needlepoint and watercolor prints. Creative Teaching Press used the Marque doll on cards, stickers and writing paper, and I receive a small royalty from them. I have written two magazine articles about the Marque doll, with photos of both dolls.

There is no reason these ideas could not work for you a hundred times over on a smaller scale with a good but less-valuable doll.

BOOTS TYNER

Boots Tyner had the talent and education to do many things. She gave up a secretarial job to make portraits-of-children dolls. She was such a perfectionist that it took a long time; she made almost nothing her first year. A few years later that all changed. Her husband's business talents and education, combined with hers, turned her doll business into a fast-growing success.

Today, Boots makes molds (to sell) from children models instead of portraits. When you see Boots Tyner's booth at a doll show, there is always a line of people waiting to buy molds of her delightful children.

Ingredients to Make Your Business a Success

Along with a good product or idea, other ingredients are needed to make a project a financial success and to help you feel good about it once you've done it.

First, you must set goals; sometimes you must reset your goals. Consider short-term goals and long-term goals. Say to yourself, "I will make so much, sell so much, do so much by a certain date," then work toward accomplishing your goal! It takes determination to be successful with dolls or anything else.

You must work longer and harder than anyone else, and you must be organized so every effort counts. Aim in one direction only, even in small things.

A good rapport with others in the field is essential. In the doll world, financial success cannot be built by one person working alone. Success includes the cooperation of thousands to whom, or for whom, you are selling, writing or producing.

Honesty is important—it can make or break your dream of success. Knowledge of dolls is essential, but this can be learned. Talent is a useful ingredient, which can be expanded to its fullest in the doll world.

Be alert to what you already have to begin with, such as a doll collection, special knowledge, talent, special space or ideas.

A willingness to share and help others is also necessary in the field of dolls. Maybe I should have put this ingredient first. Because my own success came almost entirely from sharing, I feel very strongly about this trait and its place in the doll business.

TOOLS YOU'LL NEED

Integrity and dependability in the doll world are tools that lift us to the level we desire; they are the kind of tools that make giants out of ordinary people. These special tools work like a car jack—they let you lift what would otherwise be impossible. A sense of humor and a smile are smaller tools that will help you many times over.

Left: Kiddie cars, tricycles and wagons are made in doll sizes. These help collectors set dolls in lifelike scenes. It takes a fine craftsman to produce an item like this. Doll is Simon & Halbig.

Jed Selby with Maynard John, his Cabbage Patch Kid. Popularity of these dolls was due to an incredibly successful and effective advertising campaign.

You may be surprised; you'll get back what you give—multiplied. Doll people with whom you're associated mold you or you mold them. Your mind is colored, like a dyer's hands, by what you associate with.

In working with dolls, it's easy to think you're working with things, but to be really successful, you must work with people. People will judge you and your products. It is they who will like or dislike you. Think *people,* not only things or products.

Fear can be an asset. Fear of failure comes most often because of lack of preparation or lack of knowledge. Let your fear increase your desire to work harder. Fear that is out of control can cause destruction of the entire doll business you have built. Your fear must be controlled and recognized, and even appreciated.

Practice solving problems. Figure out how to do something better. Decide how you can accomplish a job more quickly and more efficiently. Maybe there's a better way. This type of creativity comes more easily if you practice it.

Perseverance is something we must all be aware of. Make a practice of finishing any task you start. Don't put off or leave something half finished. I grew up with my father telling me to finish the job before I quit; it would make me feel good. It worked.

Be efficient. Keep projects at hand ready to work on at odd moments. Develop good concentration. Don't be distracted or taken away from your main task. Concentrate your efforts on things that count.

Convince yourself there is no such thing as failure, and tell yourself nothing is impossible. All doll entrepreneurs begin with self-confidence, believe they have the ability to be successful and promise themselves they will do it. A positive attitude benefits everyone involved.

I keep repeating the idea of establishing goals. This has been necessary for me. I set a goal many years ago that seemed good for me. From the first doll I made, my goal was to give the world the wonderful hobby of doll making and to add my bit to world cooperation and understanding through this universal toy—the doll. I wanted to give all I could to the doll world through books, instruction and my own research.

I'm still working toward that goal, even though I know there is no point where I'll say I have completed, finished or attained the highest point possible. There has never been any dream or thought of financial success tied to my goals.

Today, I have another goal I am striving for—to give the hard-working, diligent doll lover and doll maker all the help I can to achieve wealth or financial success for their work with dolls.

TRAINING YOURSELF

In our world today, there is a great deal of specialized training available. Specialized tapes, classes and seminars are given for department heads and salespeople. They are given self-improvement books and guides. Through this training, they are convinced they can do great things and are given a "road map" to achieve top performance.

Many of these same ideas can be used in small and large doll businesses. Everyone needs to know and apply the rules of success, which are:

1. Visualize your objective (where you want to go).
2. Determine when you expect to reach these goals.
3. Decide how you expect to get there.

Your map must be drawn, the timetable set and the objective visualized *before* you begin.

From the beginning, let successful people inspire you, but develop your own ideas. Let your imagination focus on objectives; unsuccessful people focus on obstacles. Set out with determination, and overcome your fears of failure.

DORIS FLYNN TAYLOR

Doris Flynn Taylor wrote her own story for me.

"Sometimes I think I'll wake up and find it's all been a dream. I cannot believe that in the last few years I've had such great success in the doll world. Behind every successful person there are many people who contribute to that success, and my case is no exception.

"I was given a book on making porcelain dolls that was written by Mildred Seeley; she lived in Oneonta, New York, which wasn't too far from our house. On my husband's day off, he drove me up there. By a happy mistake, we went to the Seeleys' home instead of their shop. When Mildred answered the door, I held up the book and said, 'Are you this Mrs. Seeley?'

"I must have looked like a lost puppy because she took pity on me and invited us into her beautiful home without a moment's hesitation. Surrounded by priceless dolls, she spent the afternoon showing me how to pour molds, set eyes and do the mechanics of doll making. Mr. Seeley and Ed discussed kilns and mold making. When I left I said, 'Please don't be so quick to let strangers into your home again. We could have turned out to be Bonnie and Clyde.'

"Mildred explained when she was starting in the doll business there was no one to help her, so she vowed she would always be willing to help others get started. She certainly has kept her word. On her advice, I took some seminars at the Doll Artisan Guild to learn how to make reproduction dolls.

"When my husband died in 1979, I thought my world had ended, but my interest in dolls kept me going. After a trip to the Orient in 1980, I took a Maggie Head Kane seminar in sculpting. I didn't want to learn how to sculpt, but I had 11 of Maggie's dolls, and this was the only way I could meet her. I had never sculpted before, but the Hakka Woman doll was the result of my experience in her seminar.

"In 1982, I traveled back to Kam Tim, Korea, the home of the lady I used as a model for the Hakka Woman doll and gave her a doll. In July 1985, I returned and gave her a book I had written in which she is featured.

"My doll has sold beyond anyone's expectations. I have since sculpted 10 other Oriental originals. My dolls have taken me to the Orient four times and to Europe when the dolls were exhibited at the Global Doll Conventions in Lucerne, Switzerland.

"I'm grateful for the success I have achieved, but I hope I never forget I could not have done it alone. I'm lucky I was able to bring forth a talent I didn't even know I possessed, at a time in my life when I desperately needed something to hang onto. My dolls gave me a new life when my old one came crashing down around me. I consider myself very fortunate indeed!"

Doris Taylor's Oriental dolls. Read her detailed "Dollionaire" story on the previous page about how she began to create these uniquely beautiful dolls.

You'll soon know the joy of financial independence through dolls.

Strength to go forward or to recover after a setback comes from within. You must believe in yourself. It will help if you keep your word and follow through as you say you will. Form good habits, and think big. Procrastination is the path to failure.

Believe in what you can do and accomplish. My mottos are "Do it now!" and "Make it happen!" In 1978, I decided we should have an International Convention of the Doll Artisan Guild (DAG). I made it happen. At a dinner party for doll judges and other important people in the doll world, I asked if people thought it should be done the next year. They all agreed, but the head of the Guild said a convention could not be planned and carried out in less than a year's time. We all assured him it could, and it was. That convention, and the conventions that have followed, have all been great successes.

The following ideas will help you make your plans a reality. Use these ideas to make things happen in *your* life.

1. You must have the *desire* to succeed, and you must have the desire to do a great job. Establish exactly what you want to achieve and what you will give in return.
2. Have *faith* in yourself. Convince yourself you can do whatever you set your mind to, and eliminate all negative thoughts.
3. *Persistence* is a way to success. When going gets tough, be persistent in your efforts. It takes courage to persist when things go wrong. Don't stop trying, and don't give up.
4. A *plan* is necessary. It maps the way to go and keeps you on a straight course.
5. *Knowledge* of dolls (the more extensive the better) is extremely important. Train your mind, advance your education and grow.
6. Establish and use *good habits*. Good habits are essential to a successful business venture.
7. *Enthusiasm* is contagious. Be enthusiastic

about your work, your service or your product. Do your job with enthusiasm and a smile, and you'll get it all back, doubled. Don't expect others to be enthusiastic about your product if you aren't.

8. It's important to share your doll ideas with others who have the *same interests*. You need a sounding board and a testing place for ideas. Interested people will stimulate you and your thinking. They will help you reach your goals faster. Be careful when selecting this group—one pessimist can ruin it. Often family members are good sounding boards; I always use my husband and my children. Have council, but make up your own mind.

9. *Decision-making*, or lack of it, can make or break you. Take time to study a situation, then make your decision. Make up your own mind, and stick with it.

10. *Specialized knowledge*, which is developed through work or education, can be one of your biggest assets when establishing a doll business. It will give you power and direction and provide methods to bridge weaknesses. Knowledge of your field can be expanded with courses, self-study and by associating with people who are knowledgeable.

Anything you can dream up, you can achieve. People are made that way. You can also think up ideas of how something can be done better.

Children's chairs and other antique furniture are good-selling items in a doll shop. Sell these items in your shop to help boost sales.

CREATIVITY AND HOW IT WORKS

Creative people try to come up with something original or new, such as a new idea. Creative people love problems that need a solution, and they enjoy being creative.

For most creative people, solving a problem or dreaming up something new is the ultimate pleasure, and any work this may involve is fun.

Psychologists believe creative potential can be stimulated by practice; you can *learn* to be something you thought only a few lucky people could be. Creativity is a sudden inspiration, a spark of light, a bright idea, a solution to a problem or the creation of something new. We all dream, and when we work at it, we can create solutions. Many of us don't try because we don't believe we can be innovators.

JOYCE JUSTUS

Justus Dolls are the creation of artist-craftsman, Joyce Justus. Her sculptured fabric figures show meticulous attention to detail and quality. Each figure has individual facial characteristics created by handstitching or needle sculpture. Bodies are built over armatures and covered with hosiery "skin." The entire doll is made by the artist. Many are three-dimensional portraits that combine craft and art.

Making money with dolls is an area in which creative people fare well. They are constantly coming up with new dolls, new products and new ways to keep doll collectors happy. In the doll world, the key isn't being brilliant—it's using your creativity as a skill.

Creativity can be sharpened with practice. The most important thing is to believe in yourself—believe you *can* do anything you set your mind to. Then do it!

AMBITION

Having ambition for yourself is not a sin—nor is it a sin for your family or your doll club. To work, plan, set goals and be ambitious is to achieve.

Often jealous people label an ambitious person as pushy, but this is not necessarily so. To be ambitious and get ahead, a doll collector, doll maker or doll club does not need to tread on anyone's toes. There is room for many types of ambitions in the field of dolls.

In doll clubs, some people become jealous when a club constantly pushes ahead doing wonderful, creative things. Jealousy enters into the picture because some clubs lack the leadership, inspiration and ambition to be creative. Ambition leads to creativity, and creativity leads to enjoyment.

AGES OF THE SUCCESSFUL

In many professions, jobs or hobbies, we find a certain age group is more adaptable or more successful than another. I have surveyed the doll world for many years, and I have found the age range of those involved is amazing. I have found success and happiness in a young person selling her first dolls or doll products. That same happiness is apparent in a retired man or woman tending their table at a convention or doll show.

The doll world welcomes anyone with creativity or expertise, no matter what age. At doll conventions, there is always a place for the daughter of a doll collector. In the following years, we often see that daughter at her own table, following in her mother's footsteps.

Young people often have their own doll ideas. On the opposite page I have described the little wood "Colleen dolls." It is one story of a young girl starting out in the doll business. Some teenagers paint dolls and outshine adults with their exquisite brush control. Some children have grown up in their mother's doll studio and produce work almost as good as their mother's. One case in point is the beautiful work of P.J., the daughter of Pam Lembo.

We also find elderly men and women attending a convention to sell antique dolls as their once-a-year outing. For some, a doll convention is their only exposure to the public. The rest of their business is conducted by mail or over the telephone. They are extremely successful and have been making money for years. These are people who know old dolls and the fortune that can be made buying and selling them. They are also aware of the friendships and happiness that has come to them through dolls.

Hundreds of doll studios across the country are managed and classes are taught by men and women from 20 to 60 years old. It is their technique and the way they care for students that counts, not their age. Studio teachers span all ages with success.

Seminar teachers must be able to get around easily, be able to travel, have no young children to leave behind and be able to withstand the rigors of travel and motel living, along with a full schedule of teaching. Many successful seminar teachers do well, and they are excited about their good fortune.

Many women in doll businesses were trained in specific fields, such as teachers, historians or artists. They spent time raising their children, but they still had the urge to do something. They entered the world of dolls later in life and found their places; many also found wealth and an exciting new life.

Dolls were not a big field for men of any age until recently, when men began to see the money and profits connected with doll businesses. At first, only a few older men sold antique dolls. Today, younger men are exhibiting reproduction dolls for sale, as well as antique

COLLEEN SEELEY

My daughter, Colleen, was 8; her brother Jay was preparing for the annual Woodside Fair—at 10 he managed and advertised it. The fair allowed children to earn pocket money and have the experience of selling, making or doing something. Colleen had nothing to sell, so she came up with the idea of painting little dolls on 2-inch wood forms that looked similar to the tops of clothes pins. She added bits of felt for hats and yarn for hair.

Colleen made a collection of farmers, ladies with aprons and little girls with braids. She had exceptional coordination, and the dolls were good from the start. They sold quickly. Someone from the Farmer's Museum said they might sell a few at the museum if she took some up to show. The lady at the museum said, "We'll take a gross to start." Colleen turned to me and said, "How many are a gross?" She went home to make 144 more little dolls.

As time passed, she made 20 standard designs and many special ones. She sold them to The Farmer's Museum, in Cooperstown, New York, the Sturbridge Village Museum, in Sturbridge, Massachusetts, and the Colonial Williamsburg Museum in Williamsburg, Virginia. She saved her money for college. She did this all through junior high, high school, Cornell University and her master's program at Michigan State University. She had more than she could do, so she enlisted my aid and finally her father's help. When she got her master's degree, she said, "I quit," with a $4,000-doll order in hand.

But this was not the end of "Colleen's Dolls." The idea, patterns, paints and materials were given to her cousin, Jeanne, who now makes delightful dolls and sells them at juried craft shows all over New England.

dolls. A few younger men with art training are teaching modeling of original dolls. One example is Lewis Goldstein, who teaches how to make original dolls at seminars held around the country.

I know of several cases in which a man left his regular 8-to-5 job to promote his wife's dolls or has helped run a financially successful doll studio. Mary Stevens' husband, Steve, a sales representative for a large company, now works full time for her. Boot Tyner's husband, Charlie, an engineer, took a leave of absence for a year to promote her original portrait dolls.

Other men, who manage large firms, have added dolls for their companies to sell or added large departments for selling and promoting limited-edition dolls. These are men of all ages, perhaps at the height of their money-earning careers.

Other men have turned to the auction field to sell other people's dolls. This seems to be one of the best fields in which men can earn money with dolls.

Dolls are one of the best areas of work and fulfillment for a handicapped person. Many types of doll work can be accomplished by even an extremely handicapped person. Age has no bearing on their income ability. We have wood carvers, doll-head modelers, doll makers, doll collectors and doll sellers who are handicapped, and they all enjoy the world of dolls.

The ages of men and women, or even children, seem to have no bearing on their success in doll businesses. Financial success can come at any age, unlike many other businesses or occupations.

Success doesn't always mean financial success. It might mean giving something worthwhile to the world, contributing something to world understanding or it could be a Millie Award or a blue ribbon. It is being happy doing something you like to do.

Making Your Doll Business Work for You

Many creative aspects of the doll world—doll making, making doll-related items or writing about dolls—often start out as a hobby. It might be something to do after work or on the weekend for enjoyment and relaxation. It could be totally unrelated to your job or profession.

If you are in this kind of situation, you may have begun to spend more of your spare time working with dolls. Maybe you took a table at a Saturday doll show, just for fun. Suddenly, your hobby began to show some profit, and you realized you had created a *second job* for yourself. This is the way it begins for many people.

A second job can also be deliberately planned. It can be a fun way to use evenings, mornings, Saturdays and Sundays to earn extra income, or it can be a way to exercise your creativity. It could give you a chance to try something new or to try many new things without giving up the security of your present job.

A second job, using your talents in the doll world, will give you a chance to test a new hobby or test your talents. It could help you evaluate your own management abilities or business skills.

This "other" job could also give you a chance to practice or enhance your professional skills. It could give you more self-confidence or help move you into a new career. It could be the path to independence that you've been searching for.

If a second job can't support you, eliminate it and try something else. It's not as though your entire income depended on it. You can take years to test it, if you wish.

A second job in dolls can often make you financially independent. It can ease your money situation and contribute to the support of your family without you having to risk leaving your present career. In time, it can also allow you to leave an uninteresting job or a job you dislike.

Left: Some people teach handsewing and hold 2- and 3-day seminars about things you need to know to sew doll clothes by hand. Teachers usually sell materials, needles and items needed to create a finished product. Rosemary Post is one of these teachers. Doll is Hilda on toddler body; dress is handsewn but not labeled as to maker.

Long-Faced Jumeau belonging to Marshal Martin. We wonder—is Marshal a teacher with a second job in dolls, or would he prefer to work in dolls full-time? Dolls put him through college.

You may receive psychological rewards from a job working with dolls, and it may give you a feeling of independence and a sense of pride. All second-job workers in the doll business love their work—it is chosen above all other work. It's wonderful when your money-earning second job is something you would do for fun. Jackie Jones, a doll-hat maker says, "I get paid for doing this—the thing I love most to do."

With a second job in dolls, you'll make many wonderful friends. You'll make useful contacts, and lifelong relationships.

A job in dolls can also be a job you keep doing for extra income after you retire. Many people in the doll world have made more money in their retirement doll business than they did in an 8-to-5 job they had for a lifetime. Dolls are especially adaptable to the over-60 age group, as you will discover when I discuss various jobs.

A second job with dolls might help you make more money, but it isn't a lazy person's way to riches.

TO BE A SUCCESS

Working with dolls takes hard work, study, research and time. It may not be easy, but it will be fun and rewarding. Some important things you need to be a success with dolls include:

1. Be well-organized—with your time and your business dealings.
2. Be a good manager—plan ahead to achieve the goals you set for yourself.
3. Feel satisfaction in the job you do.
4. Have family cooperation, commitment and understanding.

You may want to keep your doll business separate from your other job. It may be best not to disclose you have another job. Keep them separated, or the second job could jeopardize your main job.

You may want to give yourself 1 year or 5 years to test your second job to see if you want to give up the first job. You'll know when it's time to leave the first job because the job in dolls will be occupying your thoughts, and you'll resent the time spent away from the dolls. Your doll career will become the most important thing to you.

If the second job in dolls doesn't work, it could be for one of many reasons. Read the list below, and see if any of these situations apply to you.

1. The idea was too large to carry out.
2. You didn't spend enough time on your plan; it was poorly prepared.
3. You started too big.
4. It wasn't a practical idea.
5. You committed too much time or money without a plan.
6. You spent too much time doing the part you liked best and let other necessary things slide.
7. There wasn't a market for the item.
8. Effective exposure was missing.
9. The quality of your product was lacking.
10. You didn't have clear goals to work toward.

DONNA TURNER

Donna's What Knot seemed a very appropriate name for the shop and work of Donna Turner, a crocheter of doll fashions. Donna crochets costumes for small dolls and custom designs costumes for special dolls. She has many dresses and accessories available for sale at doll shows. She also crochets socks similar to the ones antique French dolls wore.

Donna writes, "I learned the art of crocheting when I was 9, along with quilting and embroidery. I can crochet and design costumes without a pattern. My first big chance came in 1981, when I was asked to make some native American dolls. These were sold at the Heard Museum in Phoenix. In 1983, I was selected to show with the top artist of the state of Arizona. I find making doll costumes a challenge."

Sue Solomon's miniature dolls are unusual. Sue studied costume design and now does it in miniature. She also costumes dolls for other people.

If things don't work out the way you planned in personal fulfillment or money, don't give up. Before you decide to quit, seek professional advice about the aspect of the business that is going poorly. You may find the help you need from this book or from a business consultant. You may need legal or professional help, or you may need specific training or education to improve what is lacking.

ADVANTAGES TO A SECOND JOB IN DOLLS

There are special advantages to a second job in dolls. Many things you would normally buy become tax deductible, and this can help reduce your taxes. Think of the fun of traveling all over the country to doll shows; this could be tax deductible. Travel related to dolls and your business may be deductible, so check with your tax adviser.

All the supplies you use in a doll-related business are deductible, whether it is film for photography, material for doll dresses or paper and materials for building something.

If your entertainment is doll related, some portion of this may be deductible. Equipment, such as molds, that is necessary to carry out your business is deductible. If it is large equipment, such as a kiln, it can be depreciated.

An office in your home and your work space, if not used for anything else, can be a great help for tax purposes. A certain portion of your home—a ratio of the size of the house and space used for business—can make a basis for deductible utilities and depreciation. For example, if your office takes 1/8 of the total house space, 1/8 of the taxes and utilities are deductible. You can also depreciate 1/8 of your house. Total deductions cannot exceed the gross income that resulted from the use of your second job in dolls.

If you are a mold maker and purchase a doll to make a mold of its head and body, you can depreciate the cost of the doll over a 5-year period. Further education in the field of dolls

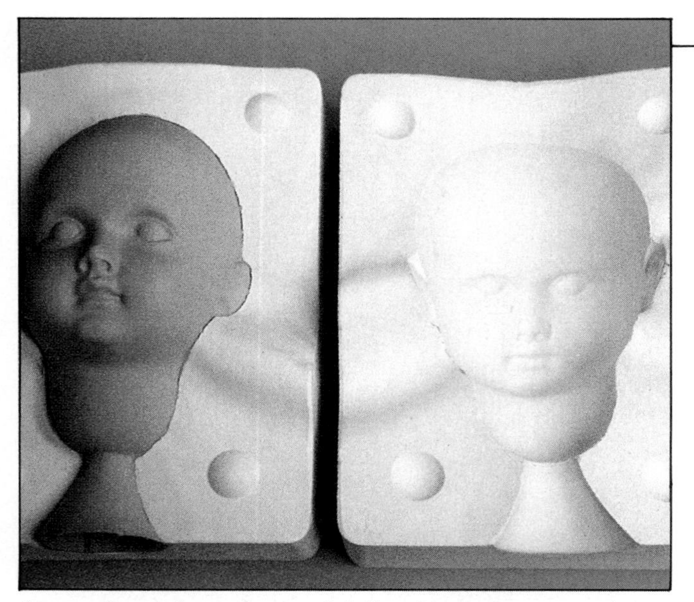

Above: Carefully made, good doll molds are money makers.

Below: Christmas stocking by Barbara Elmore, who is just getting started in the doll business. For this stocking, she used a picture of our A.T. that we named Stephanie.

may also be deductible. Before you do anything, *always* check with your tax accountant!

There may be other doll-related expenses or items that can be depreciated or deducted. Be sure to check out every angle.

A job in dolls has many advantages besides saving on taxes. It may become more than just a way to help make ends meet financially. It might enhance your present career or let you explore a more appealing alternative.

A doll career as a second job presents a challenge. This career gives you a chance to do something creative. Dolls may give you a chance to use your talents, experience or education. Dolls as a second job is something that can be done without taking too big a chance.

A second job in dolls can give you a chance to take your ideas to the marketplace. It allows you the opportunity to make your plans work. A second job provides a testing time and gives you a chance for your talents and creativity to work. It can change a hobby into a profitable enterprise. In general, a job in dolls can be an inexpensive proving ground for your ideas.

SELF-EMPLOYMENT OR REGULAR EMPLOYMENT?

There is usually more than one direction you can go to be successful. Careful forethought and planning can sometimes determine whether self-employment or employment by someone else is the best alternative for you.

If you are self-employed, you must be a self-starter and motivated from within. You must get yourself to work in the morning with no time clock to punch. You must use your working hours to get necessary things accomplished. To many self-employed people, setting their own hours is one of the greatest advantages of working for themselves.

Self-employment makes you the boss, with all the decisions to make. All the problems of money, production, employment or sales are *yours!*

If you relish solving problems, working long hours, seeing your business grow and can accept and correct your own mistakes, then perhaps self-employment is for you.

Once you've decided you're the type to run your own doll business, there are other things to consider.

- You must decide if you have an idea, a talent, a collection, education, experience or skill from which you can start and build a business.
- Determine if there is a market for your product.
- Check to see if similar businesses have been successful or if they have failed. Try to discover why they succeeded or did not. If they were successful, find out how long it took.
- If necessary, decide on a suitable location for your business.
- Find out about whatever kind of help your business may need and where you can get the help if you need it.
- Think about how much cash is needed to start the business, and decide if you have enough or can get a loan. This is discussed in more depth on page 43.

Many successful doll businesses started at a kitchen table. Some have been financially successful without having the overhead of a store. These types of businesses have been in four fields—the antique doll seller, the doll maker, the doll teacher and the accessory-or-clothing maker, such as shoe making, wig making or costuming.

Other people have had big ideas, and they were aware of their own talents. They went out and borrowed money, rented a shop for a doll studio or store and built a business on dolls. Since 1982, I have discovered many men who have quit well-paying jobs to assist their wives in selling, promoting, teaching, traveling, pouring molds or making molds. Often, two can do a job better than one, and many couples enjoy working together.

Many of these successful people were not young when they started their "doll careers." They had raised their families but still had the urge to do something in the business world. Their success rate seems to have little to do with their age.

NANCIE LUTZ

Nancie Lutz, of The Doll Works, publishes and edits the *Doll Directory*. This is no small accomplishment. The book has about 230 pages, including different kinds of information, such as a list of publishers, list of periodicals, doll associations, doll museums and doll advertisements. Nancie has attempted to list all established doll-world businesses in the United States, and she doesn't charge for listing but sells her directories to anyone who is interested.

Nancie is a long-time doll maker, but it was her experience in library research and working on reference books that gave her the tools to make her series of *Doll Directories* professional and successful.

Many doll conventions give out bags to everyone who registers. Designing these bags could be a good business to start for someone who is housebound.

The majority of doll businesses have been run with common sense—no study of business procedure was made prior to the beginning of the business. Apparently, it can still be done that way. I am also aware of several home businesses that have been taken over by skilled, business-educated executives.

Many small businesses have grown into multimillion-dollar doll industries. It's hard to tell if it happened because of the sturdy, honest, well-established foundation on which the businesses were built or the executives' management skills.

Before you choose self-employment, you must first analyze yourself, then your situation. The amount you earn in dolls can be better controlled and often times bigger than a salary from an 8-to-5 job. The main thing in working for yourself is that you're doing what you enjoy doing. Sometimes the job is something you would be doing even if you weren't getting paid.

DOLL BUSINESS AT HOME

Dolls, doll-related items, doll writing and doll photography are a few ideas for home businesses. These doll businesses can be done in a home, in apartments and townhouses. Some successful ones operate out of garages, laundry rooms, basements and even barns.

A home-based doll business usually involves the entire family. It doesn't matter if mother uses the business for full-time work or father uses it as part-time employment; the whole family must cooperate and join in the "production." Even with a one-person job like writing, cooperation is needed when the dining-room table is filled with piles of paper and pictures, and no dinner is ready. There are times when the home business won't let you keep a regular schedule.

The doll entrepreneur must talk to, discuss with and listen to the family concerning the doll business. In the beginning, and beyond, you must explain how the job and income will affect family members. Explain what part the family will play in the desired end results.

A family home business is a wonderful way to teach children about money and responsibility. Many successful businessmen grew up in small businesses. Many doll businesses are appropriate for children, and children find the work intriguing.

A home business gives you the chance to be boss, even if it only expands your hobby. It gives the homemaker a chance to earn while remaining at home.

Keep careful records. In the September 1985 issue of *Money Magazine,* it was reported that 13% of all households in the United States run some sort of business from the home. More women are not just dreaming of a home business—they're doing it with success and happiness! Some businesses are part-time or expanded hobbies, but many are full-time operations that provide much of a household's income.

There are advantages to operating out of your home. The greatest is holding down expenses; it's a lot less expensive to run a business out of your home than it is to operate a store. Operating from your home saves you rent. It lets you build up a business gradually. It saves commuting money and clothing money. You won't have to hire a baby sitter because you'll be at home with your children. You can still run your house while you run your business.

INGREDIENTS FOR SUCCESS

There are some things you need to succeed in a home business. Before you really decide if you want a business at home, check your own abilities, and see how a home business will affect the rest of your family.

Below are some questions to ask yourself before you seriously consider running a business out of your home.

- Do you have the ambition and drive to start work and know what has to be done? You must be a self-starter.
- Are you creative? Can you solve problems? There will be many problems involved in whatever doll endeavor you choose. You *must* be able to solve your own problems.
- Can you work alone, maybe all day?

- What will you do with friends or neighbors who don't believe you are really working and drop in at odd hours?
- Do you have a sense of humor so you can laugh at your mistakes and correct them?

Another big consideration to think about before you go into a home business is the demand for your product. Consider the following requirements:

- Is your idea or your product in demand? Can you create a demand for it?
- Do you know how to advertise and sell your product?
- Is the product or service one that will continue to sell over the years?
- Can you build a line of products around your idea?
- How will you sell your product? Will you produce a catalog or sell through advertisements in doll magazines?
- How much competition is there in your line of work?
- What special thing do you have that will make customers come to you? Stay with you?

You must know whom your customers are and whom your potential customers are. You can learn a great deal if you listen to them.

LYNDA AND ALAN MARX

Lynda and Alan Marx sell their reproduction bisque dolls at large shows. They work full-time at doll making. I tried to get a photograph of the booth at a recent UFDC Convention, but it was impossible because the booth was so full of buyers. Their dolls are beautiful in workmanship and costume. Lynda used her inborn talents to develop her skills. This combination, along with her husband's business skills, make their on-going business a success.

Selecting hard-to-find, rare, imported silks and laces from France is the job of Janice Naibert. Availability of these items can make doll couturiers very happy. This photo was taken at the 1985 UFDC convention in Atlanta.

TYPES OF DOLL BUSINESSES

Think of the hundreds of home businesses connected with dolls, such as appraising dolls, doll-business consultant, doll-fashion consultant, costuming, repairing, shoemaking, photography, writing, bookkeeping for other doll firms. The types of businesses run at home can be broken down into four categories—product sales, craft or handwork enterprises, writing, and bookkeeping and services.

Talk with people in similar businesses or situations. Attend small-business seminars held by business colleges or community colleges. Learn as much as you can about how to start a small business *before* you jump into it.

Talk to professionals or an accountant about how to set up your books. They know all the legal aspects of a home business. Write down your goals, plans and objectives so you can see them and discuss them with your family.

The Small Business Administration (SBA) was set up to help small businesses get started. The SBA has many pamphlets available, gives good advice and will back a loan. See your yellow pages for the address and telephone number of the nearest SBA. A list of some SBA publications appears on page 122.

PRICING YOUR PRODUCT

From the beginning, one of the most important things to know is how to price your product. Pricing a homemade item is very difficult. You must consider and add into the price the following things—the time (your hourly wage) it takes to make the item, cost of materials, cost of space in the house, some portion of utilities, your car, the time it takes to prepare advertising materials, answer letters, pay bills and any extra tasks you perform. Everything must have a price on it—especially your time. Valuing your time will help you make money.

In the beginning, you need to do some projecting. How long can you go without making a profit? How many items will you have to sell each month or year to make a profit? How much will advertising cost? Beginners often make the mistake of selling things at a price that is too low. They fail to figure all the costs, or they want to build up trade, then increase prices. This doesn't usually work. Charge a fair, competitive price from the beginning.

Setting the price for a doll service is more difficult. For example, if you decide to start a business repairing old dolls, people want to know how much it will cost to repair a doll *before* you do the job! If you've been in the business for years, you know by looking at a doll approximately how long it will take to repair it, how much a new leg will cost and how much it will cost to make a new costume. You can give the owner an estimate right on the spot.

A newcomer could underestimate the time or costs. The greater the skill that is necessary and the greater amount of training and more practice you have had, the higher the price you can charge.

YOU CAN CARE FOR YOUR CHILDREN

According to statistics, almost half of the children under 6 in the United States have working mothers. Some children stay with relatives. Many are cared for in day-care centers, and some have baby sitters.

It's difficult to find and be able to afford quality day care for young children. It's difficult for a mother to turn her children over to someone who may be less-educated and less-qualified in child care than she is. Many women want to make decisions and train and teach their children themselves. Many mothers do not want to miss their children's formative years.

Good printed patterns to fit dolls are necessary for most doll seamstresses. Consider using your talents and working for someone else.

This is where a home business in dolls might help. You save the cost of day care and can make more than minimum wage. If you prefer to care for your own children, train them and be with them while you "work" at home, dolls might be for you.

WORKING FOR SOMEONE ELSE

You may have a special talent, such as designing dolls, yet you hate the thought of trying to sell what you've made. Maybe you're a writer and want to write. If you're a wig maker and have no desire to advertise, you may not sell your products.

You and others can benefit from your skill and expertise by finding employment in a doll concern that will let you work at the job you like, and let the company do the worrying for you. Doll concerns need many workers, from doll designers to advertising copywriters. Many companies employ mold makers, painters, secretaries, salesmen and teachers—almost any job you could possibly desire.

These jobs are usually 8 to 5, with hourly pay. When you go home, you can forget the job and not worry about it. Your paycheck will come, your health insurance will be covered and your retirement planned for.

Doll companies vary in the number of people they employ and how their workers are treated. Some doll-making firms are like factories; others are like stores or studios. In a factorylike place, you may do only one small task all day long, such as putting the head on a doll. In a studio-type place, you might paint faces or complete an entire doll.

There are jobs in dolls somewhere between self-employment and regular employment. I know of many women who have found this the ideal situation. In these types of jobs, there are many variations, but the situation is similar to the "cottage industry" in which people are employed to do piece work.

REWARDS AND EMPLOYEE RELATIONS

Some companies, and their employees, are dreaming up novel ideas and rewards for top distributors. Diane Anderson, employed by Kemper Tools, had a wonderful idea—a cruise. The company gave their top 10 distributors an all-expense-paid cruise for two for a week. Five other shops were each awarded $250, and five additional shops got $100 each.

Employer-employee relations can often make or break a business. It doesn't matter if the business is small, with only two employees, or whether it's a giant with hundreds of employees. The most important thing is for an employer to think of employees as people. Think of them as people with problems and ideas. Many employers think only about profits. They don't set up work hours, vacation times or breaks with a particular employee in mind. They prefer a machine. But these "machines" (as all *successful* employers agree), work better if oiled with a little attention and kindness.

I was visiting Duncan Ceramics many years ago. As I was talking with Bob Duncan, the president, his secretary came in with a memo. Bob excused himself for a moment, and over a loudspeaker system wished happy birthday to several employees. He also mentioned how long these people had been with the company. Bob came back to us and said he did this almost every day, mentioning births, marriages and special accomplishments.

Some employers never give their employees credit for ideas that are incorporated into the business. They collect the ideas and use them,

JAMIE ENGLERT

Jamie Englert calls her dolls *Tomorrow's Treasures,* and indeed they will be. She paints her dolls to perfection and costumes them with silks, roses and good taste. Jamie starts with an idea, then creates a doll to fill it. Once she took one of my books and made reproduction dolls in exact copies of the various dolls and costumes. Most of her dolls and costumes are created in her mind. People stop and study her dolls, then buy them! Her dolls seem to be a bit of perfect fantasy that pleases most doll collectors.

then say, "It had occurred to me to do just that." Employees will come up with valuable ideas if they are encouraged and rewarded. Incentives are like bait for ideas; good employers know how to use them.

Workers also have problems. I remember once giving an employee money to have his wife's front teeth fixed. She was a singer, with bad front teeth, and she needed to get them fixed.

Another fond remembrance, which was a tremendous hit in our family, was a special birthday remembrance for our daughter Colleen. She was celebrating her 9th birthday with a party when a telegram was delivered, addressed to *Princess Colleen*. The telegram came from a large company for whom we were distributors. The president of the company and his wife visited our shop and home at least once a year. They were aware of our family as well as our business. The lovely thought and warm wishes made a hit with Colleen and her birthday guests.

I know one company that gives out pins with jewels in them for years of service. Another company gives new fathers 3 days off with pay after their baby is born. Employees must be treated as friends and real people if a business wishes to be successful.

Important to good relationships between boss and worker are the extras, such as a pension plan or a good retirement plan that works. Good health plans are also important to a worker's happiness. Daily things, like comfort in the work place, helps keep employees happy.

In summary, I'd like to reiterate—an employer must make his employees feel important, whether they are vice presidents or custodians. The employee must feel his job is worthwhile. To be happy, an employee must feel he is contributing to the success of the company. The employer must give praise for work and rewards for things and ideas out of the ordinary.

THE SALES REPRESENTATIVE

Some producers of fine dolls use a sales representative (sales rep). Salesmen go from store to store in large areas selling a line of goods that is similar so they can be sold in many of the same kinds of stores.

Above and right: An entire collection of dolls on pillows. These Peruvian pillows are popular with doll collectors, and they are made in many variations. To sell unusual articles, such as these, you might need a good sales rep.

A sales rep may carry dolls with him as samples, or he may carry some to sell. He may take orders that you later fill.

A salesman may be an old hand, selling for years, or he may be new at the business of selling dolls. Many sales reps are husbands of doll makers who have appointed themselves as salesmen and do a fantastic job. Sales reps work on the basis of a percentage of sales or a commission.

You can make many fine products in the doll field, but unless you can get them on the market and sold, you can't make money. If you don't like selling and prefer to spend your time making items, consider using a sales rep.

CONSIGNMENT SELLING

I hesitate to write on consignment selling because I had some bad luck with this type of business in my early years. Consignment selling is used when the person managing a shop or store doesn't have the capital to purchase stock, such as dolls or doll items. The producer of the product takes her finished items to a store owner for display and sale. The store owner sells the item and keeps an agreed-upon percentage for herself.

This sounds good and looks good in the beginning, but it seldom works out as planned. Often the product is not properly cared for; it gets dirty when it is handled. Sometimes an expensive doll is sold, and the maker is not informed until months afterward.

From personal experience, I found it's difficult to collect your money or get your dolls back. If you go into this type of business arrangement, have a *written* contract. A written contract must include the selling price of the doll or product, the seller's commission, how long the shop will have the item or doll, and who is responsible for breakage, theft or damage.

IDEAS FOR SALESMEN

We are *all* salesmen. Every day we sell our ideas to others. Some of us are good salesmen; others are poor. Some of the essentials of a good salesman are listed below. A good salesman:

- Has the power of persuasion—the power to convince and win someone over to his way of thinking.
- Knows and understands the people to whom he is selling.
- Understands terms by which an item is sold and makes them clear and understandable.
- Convinces the buyer he will receive pleasure from the sale. (A sales pitch is usually more convincing than logic.)
- Convinces the buyer the profit is in his interest.
- Is friendly with potential buyers.
- Knows the doll product well, and tells the prospective buyer how it will help him.
- Convinces the buyer the product will help him reach his goal.
- Is enthusiastic about your product.

TRANSFER OF KNOWLEDGE

After studying people who have had been successful in doll businesses, I found many used their former training, their profession or their education to make their businesses successful. These professional people apply their experience and knowledge to the doll business with better-than-average success. Perhaps you can also do this.

One acquaintance used to repaint and repair cars. Today he is unable to work on cars, but he does a beautiful job of repairing and repainting old doll bodies. Another man, skilled in car manufacturing and painting, repairs bisque heads, using techniques he learned in the car business. He has a videotape on the market explaining his technique and the auto paints he uses.

A German tool-and-die maker discovered he could make doll molds in this country for a greater profit by using the same knowledge and techniques as applied to tool-and-die making. Another man worked in a furniture-making plant all his life. When it closed, he discovered he had the skill to make doll chairs, cribs and other furniture items.

A retired cabinet maker fell in love with making doll houses; it gave him an outlet to continue using his skills. A glass manufacturer made globes to display butterflies for many years. Today, his sales are greater making display cases and globes for dolls.

A ceramic company's mold maker retired early to make molds for doll heads at a higher profit. Three men who were top salesmen for large corporations quit their jobs or took leaves of absence and now work full time promoting and selling their wives' dolls.

Several of the best doll-wig makers have turned to making doll wigs after having spent

BONNIE AND LEE CAMPBELL

I searched for someone making portrait dolls of today's children, and I found the mother-daughter team of Bonnie and Lee Campbell. Bonnie writes, "My career was actually launched when I was given an art assignment in high school to make a doll. I made one in the image of my sister, Carey. I sculpted the head, arms and legs in earthenware; I still use this medium. The sculpture was fired, then painted several times. It has a mat finish.

"When the doll was finished, my teacher entered it in the National Scholastic Competition in the art-sculpture category. I won a gold medal. The doll was featured on a local television program, then sent to New York to be nationally recognized in the National Scholastic Art Exhibition. While on exhibit, Gail Zimmerman saw the doll and wrote an article about her for the *National Doll News, Omni Book.*

"After this, I made other portrait dolls. Lee, my mother, is a fine seamstress and is able to make costumes without patterns. She does all our costume design and sewing.

"Through advertising, we have found there is a market for portrait dolls. We've made portrait dolls for people all over the United States and Canada, and many customers order a second and third doll. Each doll is unique, and we spend many long hours trying to achieve the desired likeness. Also, we spend time matching materials for a costume so it looks like one the child actually wore. Our portrait dolls are made from photos.

"We love this business. It's very rewarding when we receive letters from customers saying how happy they are with their portrait doll. We thank God each day for giving us this talent."

most of their careers making human wigs. There's more money in doll wigs.

A retired Chicago hat maker gets more money for each doll hat she makes now than she did for women's hats. And doll hats take much less time and material.

A dental hygienist makes tiny sets of perfect doll teeth for use in reproduction dolls and old dolls. A leather crafter now makes doll shoes. The owner of a bridal shop makes exquisite patterns for doll costumes. A trained artist creates original dolls from real people.

A first-grade teacher and sixth-grade teacher, both retired, teach studio classes in doll making. A dressmaker applies her skills to costuming dolls. A retired window-display artist uses his talents, skills and techniques to make dolls.

These are only a few examples of people who have changed jobs and professions, and I personally have met them all. There are many more. If you're interested, talk to people at doll conventions and doll shows who have booths. It's amazing how skills from one job can be carried over into the doll field in one way or another.

THE ENTREPRENEUR

We're all entrepreneurs. Each of us does some type of business every day. If we are not selling a product, we're selling ourselves, our knowledge or our services. The more we understand this, and the more plans we make around it, the more successful we will be. Anything that has to do with dolls is our business.

At the moment, there are fortunes to be made by new doll entrepreneurs. Dolls have already produced the rich and the super-rich, but there's more. We're on the edge of a doll-business explosion.

The doll entrepreneur has many areas of doll work from which to choose. Opportunities for women are improving. The chances of a woman becoming a millionaire have increased; the number of women millionaires has nearly doubled since 1976. Many in the doll world do not wish to be counted.

There's no better time than now to decide on where and how you are going to make your fortune. There are even college courses on entrepreneurship and how to get started. One thing that has made more millionaires in the

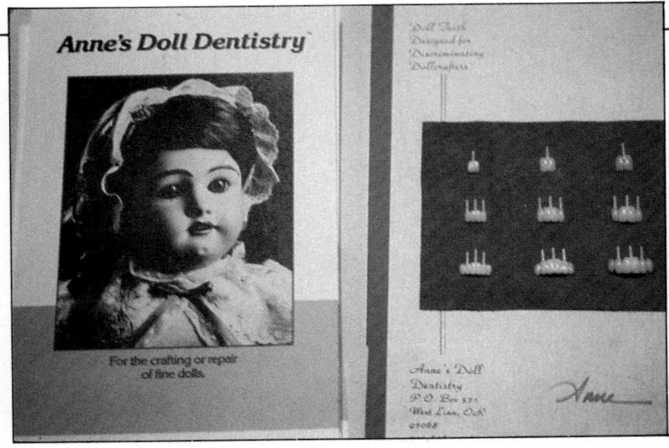

Above: One dental hygenist I know makes and sells dolls' teeth. This is an example of using knowledge about something to create a place for oneself in the doll world.

Right: E. J. dolls, like many other French dolls, have increased in value. Similar doll purchased for $300 in 1975 now sells for $3,000 or more at auction.

last few years is starting a business. The business must be built on your own idea, an unusual product, a needed product or something creative. Many of today's successful people are creating dolls or selling dolls. Study the trends, and find your specialty in the field of dolls.

For example, how about "wiring" America for dolls? Who can find a doll I've been looking for all my life or find a doll at the price I want to pay? No one has developed a computerized find-a-doll service. Think about services or products you can provide and what needs you can fill.

Even people who do not know about doll making can advise others on how to increase production, how to train for productivity and help them with time-management problems. Marketing consultants are desperately needed by a doll entrepreneur. Often a consultant understands work loads; some understand product design that can be applied to dolls. The best consultant is one with experience in all these fields.

What about spending your efforts and time with the older people helping them make dolls? Many older women love dolls and would love the opportunity to learn about dolls or work with them. Make your money working with people who will enjoy dolls and be able to pay to learn how to make them.

Consider teaching children to create and make dolls. Classes in original or reproduction doll making are almost unheard of for children. Children are naturally creative; they love dolls and would probably love to make them. Many mothers would rather send their child to a class to learn something that is fun rather than hire a sitter.

There are other things you can consider—one woman I know started and built a ceramic and doll business. It took 3 years for her to establish a profitable business, then she sold out to a large company that wanted to diversify. She held back the source of raw materials necessary for production to sell them to the plant she had sold. She made a nice profit on the sale of the business and still has the income from the sale of raw materials. She built up another sideline business in a related field, and 2 years later she sold that. Now, she has three other related businesses underway. This woman is making a great deal of money; she is one of the great entrepreneurs of our day.

Franchising—Another idea in dolls is franchising. A franchise is the right to market or provide a service as granted by a manufacturer or company. This is being done on a small scale with repairing dolls, making doll eyes and making doll wigs.

There's a tremendous amount of room for all kinds of franchises. For franchising to be successful, one ingredient is necessary. You must have a product, an idea or a method that is not available elsewhere. You must come up with something that is original, then supply the branch operations the know-how, the materials, the copyrights and printed material, along with a good company name. Think big.

BRAINSTORMING

Do you have everything but an idea? There are ways to come up with new ideas. A group of us used to get together and have a "think" session. We thought up any and every idea that we could, with no concern whether it would work or not. We listed all our ideas and hoped something practical could be worked out at a later date. Try it; you may be surprised at what will come out of one of these sessions.

Today, large companies use brainstorming to resolve problems. Specialists concentrate on a problem and attempt to solve it or circumvent it by applying what they know to something new.

This idea-creating can be used by any would-be entrepreneur. It may seem a little foolish and may not be as productive as it should be, but idea-getting multiplies many times over. The more it's used, the better it works. I believe people become idea-getters by practicing.

EXPERTISE

Along with ideas, you need to be an expert in some type of doll or doll-related area. You need to study and research until you know all there is to know about your chosen area of dolls. Research your business idea from the business standpoint; from your expertise a new entrepreneur may emerge.

CONSULTANT TO DOLL BUSINESSES

There is a need for consultants in many doll businesses, and two types of consultants are needed. The two types of consulting are *business management* and *doll expertise*. If you are an expert in either of these areas, a good business in consulting could be developed.

In a small business, knowledge of how to run an operation to make a profit, how to borrow money, money flow, cost analysis, projection of sales, credit lines, use of an accountant and keeping records are all areas a good consultant can help a doll businessperson.

A doll business also needs experts with experience in the field of dolls. A consultant may be a teacher, with a teacher's education, to advise teachers how to run seminars, conduct classes and operate a teaching studio. She might be a doll maker so she understands the problems involved in this creative process. A consultant must be able to advise customers how to improve skills, develop time scheduling, give demonstrations and teach people with varied skills in one class.

A consultant to a manufacturer of dolls or doll products needs a combination of business know-how and doll sense. This consultant could advise a businessman on how to improve painting, how to come up with a more appropriate costume or how much money to charge for a product, It could involve changing a doll business from retail to wholesale or creating better packaging of a product or improved marketing techniques.

Big doll companies use consultants all the time. Some consultants are hired on a yearly salary, as I was for Seeley's Ceramics after the business was purchased by Rolf Ericson. I worked for 6 years thinking up new ideas and outlining how they would work and affect the future of the business. I was able to help the Ericsons, who had no knowledge of dolls, turn the business into a multimillion-dollar doll-mold-and-body business. I have also seen this happen in other doll-mold businesses.

To be a consultant to a large doll business, you must have a thorough knowledge of old dolls because this forms the basic background necessary for the making of new dolls. You must have personal skills in doll making above and beyond company management. You must have the intellectual ability to cope with, and project, practical new ideas. And perhaps most important, you must have had vast experience in the field of dolls to help you make the right decisions.

To be a consultant, you must *know your subject*. You must also know how to sell it. You must have self-confidence and know, or figure out, how to market your services. To be successful, people in the doll field must make money and be happier using your advice.

There *are* ways to get started. Have a professional brochure printed discussing you and your area of expertise. Mention what you have accomplished for other companies. Include how you work, where you are located and how you helped different businesses become successful. Mention any special training you've had. Don't skimp on this brochure—it must indicate success. Have cards printed, and use the telephone to help you sell your service.

In the resource section of this book, which begins on page 119, I have listed some books that are helpful for those who want to start a consulting service.

DO YOU NEED A CONSULTANT?

There are instances when a business or art consultant could change a business from a struggling company to a money-making success. Sometimes lack of success of a company is all due to management problems, which a consultant from the outside could see. Sometimes an existing business needs the spark of a new idea to send it soaring. Sometimes a consultant can turn a business from fizzle to sizzle.

Often a person who runs a small business is so close to his business that he can't see where and when help is needed. You need to know if there are areas where you need help. If you're in this position, ask yourself the following questions to help you decide whether *you* need a consultant.

1. Do I know who my customers are, and do I know their needs?
2. Do I know what professional services are available? Where? For whom?
3. Do I know how to set up books for a business?
4. Can I cope with taxes, legal red tape and reports?
5. Can I manage my own time and get everything done?
6. Do I need a part-time secretary?
7. Do I know when to hire help and how to manage their time?
8. Do I need an answering service?
9. Do I need a better business plan?
10. Can I teach classes or seminars?
11. Can I give a perfect demonstration?
12. Do I know how to use simulated demonstrations?
13. Am I aware of available aids, such as books, videotapes, posters? Do I know how to use them?
14. If teaching doll making, have I studied old dolls?
15. How do I manage my family when I am teaching?
16. Would a "cottage industry" be a solution to my problem?
17. Will I know when it's time to move from my home workshop to a store or manufacturing plant?
18. Can I scout around for new ideas or products on my own?
19. Can I prepare an appealing, interesting selling advertisement?
20. Do I have creative ideas about promotion?
21. Do I need help with marketing strategy?
22. Am I spending too much or too little on doll shows? Advertising? Printed brochures?
23. How good a seller am I over the telephone?
24. Am I well-organized?

DIANNE DENGEL

When Dianne Dengel sat in her booth filled with dolls at the 1985 UFDC convention in Atlanta, she used every moment sewing garments for her dolls. I also saw her bringing in another load of dolls from her trailer to replenish the supply she had sold.

Dianne's dolls are large—there are children, babies, mothers, old men, grandmothers and clowns. They have painted features and soft bodies. Their charm defies description; they have a look from a different time and place. The dolls all look related, and their smiling faces reflect Dianne's childhood. See photo on the opposite page.

Dianne told me, "When I was a child, I was happy. We had a lot of freedom; sometimes we met the bus after midnight when my mother came home from work. We used to go down to the river and swim, and there were farms around with pigs. Sometimes the pigs were in swimming with us! We had a garden in back, too. Whatever we wanted for lunch, we'd pick."

Dianne makes many dolls to sell, but she is also a painter. She uses the dolls she makes as models for her paintings. Some paintings are full color, some brown and pink tones, and some just brown tones. From these paintings, she has prints made, which she also sells.

Answering these questions honestly may help you determine if you need a consultant.

When hiring a consultant, you must have complete confidence in him and carry out his suggestions. If you don't implement a consultant's ideas, you've wasted your money.

KEEPING THE MONEY YOU EARN

It's not enough to make money with dolls—you must know how to keep your money and not pay it all out in taxes. Dolls provide some fantastic ways to save money.

I have already mentioned some tax-saving tips connected with a mail-order or secondary doll business, such as travel, car, supplies, a portion of your utilities, some entertainment, some education and depreciation of your home office. In addition to these, there are great savings plans that are available to you because you're self-employed. The best is the Keogh plan.

Keogh Plan—With the Keogh plan, you can put away a percentage of gross income and not pay taxes on it or its interest until the money is withdrawn. These accounts are compounded, often paying high rates, and they grow fairly quickly. Money can be withdrawn after you reach age 59-1/2. Check with a financial planner or an accountant concerning these accounts; they're well worth the time and effort involved in setting them up.

IRAs—Individual retirement accounts (IRAs) have been well-publicized. A sum of $2,000, deposited yearly in an IRA, can build a nice retirement fund. You don't pay any tax on the money or interest until it is withdrawn. You can withdraw the money at age 59-1/2. With many IRAs, you have the opportunity to move your account so you can get the best interest or implement special investment ideas. The only thing you can't invest in is collectables.

Right: Dianne Dengel created her own dolls and methods of producing them. Dianne is a painter, and her dolls are made of canvaslike material.

Certificates of Deposit (CDs)—It takes a lot of time and study to be able to put your money in the stock market. You must be right on target at the right time to buy and sell at a profit. I find it less risky and less time-consuming to buy certificates of deposit (CDs). You must watch the interest rates and shop around for the best rate. Check the actual rate paid, not the yearly yield, and check on compounding interest. CDs are much simpler and safer than the stock market.

Bonds—There are many kinds of bonds on the market, and many are interest-free from federal taxes and some state taxes. If you buy state municipal bonds, they are also tax-free. These are not considered tax shelters, but they serve the same purpose. You earn tax-free interest, and most bonds can be resold or held until maturity.

Investing your money wisely in insured institutions is part of any money-making doll business. Money saved and used wisely can help in many ways.

Antique Dolls—Another investment must be mentioned here, and it produces great joy for any doll person. It may be the one investment that will give anyone in this field the greatest happiness. Of course, I'm talking about investing in *antique dolls*.

In the last 20 years, good antique dolls have increased in value from 15 to 20% *each year!* During short depressions or recessions, dolls have never gone down in value.

I am an investor in dolls—they are my greatest monetary asset. I feel certain when the time comes to sell them, they will do well for me.

I don't believe a collection of just any type of doll can be an investment collection. You must be selective; choose dolls that will not deteriorate and will increase in value. I suggest perfect, or nearly perfect dolls, rare dolls, beautiful dolls, marked dolls and well-made dolls. French and German bisque dolls seem to be the best investments. Today, folk dolls are becoming more popular, but many folk dolls will not last the way bisque does.

For many doll people, creating a fine doll collection is the ultimate way to save. They prefer a doll collection to money in the bank or gold bars in a safety-deposit box. It is wealth they can see each day. In return, they get enjoyment and eventually, if necessary, they can sell their investments for a profit.

Very special old costumes, along with old dolls, make up the museum of Bete Wages Advani.

INFLATION PROJECTIONS

Even though many of us read and study, we are still unsure we believe the prediction of investment newsletters. Even after we are convinced our money is going to be swallowed up by certain government actions, we still are not pushed into any preventive action.

Some forecasts have been amazingly accurate over the years in their prediction of interest rates, the rise of gold and silver, tax rates and the value of collectables.

Short-term factors or emotional reaction to rumors or events can cause investors to panic buy or panic sell. This kind of pressure could distort the trend in any collectable market. Real profit is earned on long-term investments, so we must study doll-market trends and cycles to identify what will return the highest profits.

Every day we see "doll gamblers" grabbing up dolls and doll articles for short-term resale, hoping to make a quick profit. Yet we know the careful, profitable approach of the long-time doll buyer; we see her analyzing future trends and buying for 1 year or 3 years ahead, perhaps longer.

Return on investment in dolls has never wavered. Investment in fine art and in paintings has wavered at times, and dolls could, with certain conditions, do the same thing. But they haven't to date.

Substantial profits have been earned from dolls. A careful selection of dolls for a "portfolio" may give substantial monetary returns in the years ahead. The secret is to buy *quality*. Buy dolls in the upper quarter of desirability. Even during the recession of 1980-1982, more-expensive luxury dolls were still in the highest demand.

In another of my books published by HPBooks, titled *How to Collect French Bébé Dolls*, I give specific guidelines on how to select and invest in French bébé dolls to reduce your risk and maximize your return. A few people, including me, occasionally consult over the phone or in person about particular dolls that come up for public auction or sale. Often you will find the material needed to make a proper doll selection in my books. I try to give in-depth advice I have accumulated from experience, but there is no financial genius in the doll world that is available for general consulting. The collector-buyer-seller who has made, and is making, a great deal of money keeps his methods to himself.

I often like to predict what is happening to certain types of dolls so young or new collectors can get in on the bottom floor and make more-profitable investment decisions. Between 1986 and 1990, I believe the French fashion doll, which has virtually been frozen in price for many years, will steadily increase in price and value. A few years ago, I predicted the increase in price and desirability of German character dolls. Their value and desirability increased, but I had no idea it would increase as much as it did. Many people became very successful buying and selling German character dolls.

SOURCES OF MONEY FOR START-UP CAPITAL

If an idea is good enough, if you can show its potential clearly enough and if your reputation is strong enough, you can get the money you need to start a new business or expand a small one. But you may have to try many different methods.

The most obvious thing to do is to go to your banker to try to borrow the money. Perhaps you can borrow on your home or some other piece of property. You can also try your credit union or savings and loan association.

Check family members—you may find an interest-free loan or reduced-interest loan. This is a *loan*, not a gift, and it should be accompanied by a promissory note. An older member of the family may need to invest some cash and would like to see a business grow. Or perhaps you have an affluent relative with money to loan in exchange for part of the stock.

Ask your employer—he may have money to loan. A friend of mine took his idea to his lawyer to get legal advice and ended up with the lawyer buying in!

Other Sources for Money—Borrow against forthcoming wages—this can be done at some companies. Borrow against certificates of deposit. Some people loan money and want stock, part ownership in the company or to be on the board of directors in return. You'll have to look for these investors—check newspapers under the classified section or investment opportunities. Ask your banker, and ask your friends. There are also some small business loans available—contact your local office of the Small Business Association.

You can borrow on your life insurance and still keep the insurance. Insurance pays poor dividends so little will be lost. Some companies allow people to borrow against their pension plans.

Instead of getting a big tax refund this year, figure your taxes more exactly. If you have any extra money, invest it so it can earn interest. If the government has it, it doesn't do anything for you. Plan to use your money for your business.

If the bank turns you down, ask if they have a department that loans money on new businesses. Some banks have venture capitalists who are specialists in high-risk financing.

When starting a large business, some banks have lease-financing deals in which management trades the investment tax credit and depreciation associated with the assets in return for a lower financing rate. This is a trade off that benefits the bank and your new business because you don't need the tax credit.

Bartering—Another "source" of money used today is barter. Small businesses trade services and stock with each other. An accountant can trade his services for a certain length of time for a portrait doll of his daughter. A carpenter can trade his work with a doll painter to get his store in shape. This way of working together takes a lot of imagination and creativity, but it works. I know an artist who trades his prints for dental work. Doll makers do this regularly when they trade reproduction dolls for the work of a fine seamstress.

Start-Up Capital—A would-be entrepreneur in the doll business is often stopped before she gets started because she doesn't have start-up capital. A business in its infancy needs money to get underway. Product samples must be made, marketing research and advertising done and the operation staffed.

Before you try to get money from the bank or from a family member, draw up a plan. Make a 5-year projection in costs and profits, and put it down on paper. It will help you create your plan and help you get the money you need. This is called a *prospectus*—you show it to a prospective money lender.

When You Get the Money—There are other ways to get money; some will work, some won't. Be sure you keep in mind the following *before* you sign on the dotted line.

1. Look carefully at terms before you borrow any money.
2. You may have limited choices, but shop for the best deal.
3. Use your ideas, your ambitions and your creativity to negotiate for the best deal.
4. When your business is doing well and you need more money, use your track record and your goals to help you borrow.

Making aprons is a good project for doll-club members of any age. Here my husband, Vernon, models an apron that was given to him by members of a doll club.

CORPORATIONS, PARTNERSHIPS AND SOLE PROPRIETORSHIPS

In a new doll business, there are three ways the business can be set up. You can form a *corporation*, a *partnership* or a *sole proprietorship*. This is a big decision for anyone forming a business, whether it's a mail-order business, a home business or a store. Who's the boss, who shares the profits, who gets an hourly wage—these must all be decided in the beginning to avoid problems later.

If you aren't familiar with corporations, partnerships or sole proprietorships, it's best to have them explained to you by a lawyer or accountant. Having been involved over the years in each type of arrangement, I will try to give you some personal insights.

Corporation—To form a corporation, you must involve a lawyer, and this can be very expensive. This works best in larger businesses that you expect to continue after you're dead or retired. If the business fails or goes bankrupt, it's the business, *not* your personal account, that fails. You must have at least three people involved in a corporation, and there are some tax breaks.

Partnerships—Many doll businesses are set up as partnerships. This situation is usually chosen when an item is produced by two people. An example might be a doll artist who makes beautiful dolls but who can't sew. She finds a seamstress who works well with her and understands how to costume a doll to bring out its beauty. They form a business to make and costume dolls. There are many doll companies that can be run by two people.

Family members may decide to go into partnership to run a shop and attend doll shows together. But few partnerships are successful. They may work for a short time, but few last. It's almost impossible to run anything with two bosses. Sooner or later one will feel the work is not equally divided or one partner doesn't get his share done or doesn't do it the way the other one feels it should be done.

When I look back at the experiences I've had, I advise *against* partnerships. If you have a dear friend or sister you want to work with, day in and day out, pay her as a helper and do the managing yourself. It's easier and more successful. And in this way, you'll preserve your friendship.

Sole Proprietorship—A sole proprietorship is probably best for small, new businesses. This lets you make all the decisions and all the mistakes *yourself*.

For all the business arrangements I've discussed, check with local authorities so you have the proper forms to fill out for state sales tax, licensing, zoning and all other regulations your business will fall under. There are some organizations, such as the SBA, that will help you and advise you.

Many doll businesses are "accidents" that happen without a plan or a dream. For example, a doll-hat maker makes some extra hats to take to a doll show. A friend gives her half of her table at the show. The hats all sell. The woman is delighted and cannot wait to get home to start making more hats. She doesn't know it, but she's in business for herself. I've seen this happen many times in the doll world; most of these businesses have brought financial success and happiness to the I-don't-know-anything-about-business people.

PECK-GANDRÉ

Linda Peck has always been fascinated by dolls and has a deep interest in art. She combined the two talents and became a teacher for making antique reproduction dolls. When the last of her eight children started kindergarten, she enrolled in art classes at Westminster College in Utah. Her first love is portrait painting, and she is also a very talented costume designer.

Marilyn Gandré received an art scholarship to the University of Utah, where she studied figure drawing and painting. Children are her favorite subjects, and she is an expert in watercolors. She has written and illustrated several books, done fashion illustrating and stage design. She has six daughters.

Mein Liebling, a K(star)R117 doll, was chosen by Peck-Gandré as their first in a series of large paper dolls. Their paper dolls are exact pictures of an antique doll in *every* detail. Peck and Gandré even include a beautiful paper-doll wardrobe. These are the only dolls of their kind on the market. See full-page photo on page 80.

The Mail-Order Doll Business

Having been involved in three closely related, very successful mail-order doll businesses, I have some ideas and tips to pass along that might help you. Hopefully these suggestions will help anyone already in the mail-order business and anyone planning to start a business.

A mail-order business can be a small operation or a huge corporation, with catalog sales of dolls and doll supplies. It can be a form of self-employment—as small as one person working out of his or her home. A retired person, a stay-at-home mother or a talented doll artist who has no time for a store could all put mail-order to work for them.

It is estimated that 75% of all doll business today is conducted through mail order. Some large businesses are a combination of mail order and over-the-counter business. Dolls, doll items and accessories and doll supplies lend themselves to mail-order selling.

The lure of a doll mail-order business is the thought of easy money or a chance to make it on your own with very little to start with. One doll maker's dream was to open her mailbox and find it full of money. Money, even wealth, has become a reality for many since they got into the doll mail-order business, but it didn't come without hard work and much planning.

Before you seriously consider starting a mail-order business, acquaint yourself with federal rules and regulations about selling through the mail. There are some restrictions and limitations about selling through the mail—for the protection of customers—so check *everything* out carefully before you jump into the business. Call your local postmaster—he or she can probably give you many of the details you need and refer you to others who can answer your questions.

Let's look at some of the advantages of selling through the mail.

Left: Finished costumes and pattern making all begin with designing. Finished costumes and patterns for creative dresses are available for antique dolls and reproduction dolls. Even though there were many dresses done like this one, this dress cost $88. Dress, bonnet and undies were included. Dress is by Sandra Read. Doll is a rare, early Jumeau marked only with a *J*.

For a mail-order business, a catalog is the salesman. Appealing pictures sell your products. Full-color mail-order catalogs appear in people's mailboxes each day.

1. You can reach people all over the world—you can sell to people in remote areas as well as large cities. Every doll maker or doll collector could be a potential customer. You aren't limited in the same way as you are with a store.
2. You don't need (or have the expense of) a fancy store or office. You usually have no lease or contracts if you work out of your home.
3. Advertising can usually be purchased in reasonably priced spaces in doll magazines.
4. Direct mail to a customer may be easier and less-expensive than having a store and doing local advertising.
5. You can employ part-time help or family members.
6. You and your employees can work odd hours and set your own time schedules. You can even schedule your own vacations.
7. In some states, there are tax advantages to running a mail-order business.
8. You don't have to spend time with customers who only want to browse.
9. You won't need business clothes to go to work. (There's a lot of savings here.)
10. You have complete control of your service and can make it excellent. This is one of the biggest keys to success in mail-order.
11. Anyone can run a mail-order business—women, men, young, old or disabled.
12. A mail-order business can start very small and grow larger, as demands increase.
13. A small mail-order doll business can start with little capital, so this might eliminate borrowing for start-up. It takes less investment capital than other types of business.
14. The vitality of a mail-order business depends on your national or regional advertising, not on local displays or window dressings.
15. You deal only with the postman or the telephone each day. You don't have to face the general public or deal directly with people.
16. Credit cards and toll-free numbers are not essential in the beginning, but consider adding them at some time because they do help increase sales.

MAIL-ORDER ADVERTISING

In a mail-order business, a person must be a salesperson *and* have a good product to sell. You must have ideas about what people want or need, then figure out how to make them buy it.

Some professionalism is needed in advertising. Hire an advertising agency, or talk to someone in the advertising department of a doll magazine when you advertise there. You must determine what will motivate a buyer—a photo of a beautiful doll or some convincing words concerning your patterns might do the trick.

You know what it takes to get you to put a check for $10 into an envelope for a newly developed product or to send $250 for a reproduction doll you haven't seen. The same thing that motivates you will motivate your customers, so study other ads.

Some people believe responses to an ad-

Felt dolls are becoming more popular. Modern-day felts rival the 1920s Lenci dolls, but makers must invest time and money advertising them.

vertisement are in direct proportion to the amount of money spent on the ad. With dolls, this does *not* seem to be the case, with the exception of using color for advertising a doll that is for sale. Sometimes a doll in color is so appealing that, even though we can't afford it, we will buy it.

What really matters in mail-order selling is how good the product is and how good your service is. Advertising for a mail-order business must be continuous. The minute you let down, your sales will reflect it.

One way to learn about the mail-order business is to read advertisements of other mail-order businesses. When I did a full-page color ad for my plate series, I used one large plate and five smaller plates in a row down the side. I showed the whole doll near the plate. That ad sold my plates. Within the next few months, three plate ads from other companies came out with the same format.

One rule of thumb to follow is—the higher the price of the item, the larger and more-expensive the ad must be. Consider less-expensive advertising when you begin. Use small black-and-white display ads with an eye-catching headline. This type of ad will ask the reader to send for information. When the request for information comes, mail back a fine brochure, pictures or a letter with the complete description, selling price and all other pertinent information.

Study other ads for form, language, clarity and completeness. Find ads that appeal to you, then use the format as your guide.

Pace advertising so some form of it is before the public all the time. Be prepared in advance to pay for these ads. Start small, even in doll-magazine classified ads. Then take a small display ad, and work up to a full-page advertisement in color. Some people have started the other way—with a full-page ad in color. This type of ad was used by one doll maker for a limited-edition doll, her first, and it worked.

Don't hesitate to repeat an ad that has worked for you. Make your ad appeal to doll collectors or doll makers who will read it. Experiment with different ads—not everything works every time. When you rerun an ad, change format size and copy or change photos. Use special ideas for holiday sales or special or quantity discounts. Some ads work like magic; others won't work at all.

Keep a record of what each ad does and learn from it. Code your ads and responses to them so you can tell how well each ad is received.

You might try to get free advertising in "new-products" columns that appear in many doll magazines. Any publicity you get will help your product sell; try for newspaper articles or write-ups in magazines about yourself or your doll operation. Doll directories are all right for listing your product or service, but they are only put out once a year, which isn't much help in a mail-order business.

In the doll business, it usually isn't necessary to use advertising agencies, although you may want to advertise in national magazines other than doll magazines as your company grows. Agencies can get your ads in national magazines on special pages used only in a certain regional area. Agency commissions run about 15%. This is much less costly than purchasing an ad that runs all over the country, and it gives you a testing area. Choose a good test area, such as Los Angeles or Rochester, New York.

Writing an Advertisement—When you write an ad, there are certain things it must contain.

- Name of your company
- Address and telephone number
- Name of product
- Pertinent information
- Shipping—immediate or delayed shipping (a made-to-order doll might take 6 weeks)
- Guaranteed satisfaction
- Simplified directions for ordering

The ad should be tight and space should be well-used. Use plain, easy-to-read printing. Be honest, avoid cute or tricky phrases and *never* exaggerate. Develop some copy techniques. Play up your awards or fame; many doll makers say, "I'm a Millie Winner." This alone says their doll making is excellent. Don't be modest.

Be sure there are no unclear facts or confusing directions. Use clear, appropriate illustrations to sell the product, and use bold headlines.

Don't hesitate to ask for help from the advertising department of a doll magazine if you are placing your ad there.

Be sure the doll magazine you pick is the best place to sell your product. For example, a dollmaker's magazine is *not* the place to sell a reproduction doll. Their audience is already making dolls.

Organize and keep a list of your inquiries and customers. They are valuable for direct mail with your next product. You can also purchase mailing lists for direct mailing. I have used doll lists from doll magazines; some companies sell lists for a price. Keep your list from getting too big and expensive to cover.

All mediums are used for dolls—felt, jersey, silk, porcelain, clay, various compositions. Here we have a papier-mâché "Bag Lady," by Patricia Church who teaches classes in doll making. If you were selling this doll through the mail, you'd have to include an accurate description *and* a picture!

SUGGESTIONS FOR MAIL ORDER

Mail-order businesses are easy to start on a small scale, even with a single item. If your product is good enough, you may never need another product. The product you choose to sell should be something not readily available elsewhere. Often small mail-order businesses begin by selling a homemade item. It must be a product that is not too difficult to ship, too breakable or perishable.

Many small mail-order businesses fill doll magazines with advertising and provide items a doll lover searches for.

On the following pages are some ideas and suggestions to help make your mail-order business successful. If you don't have one expensive item that sells well, work out a line of items that goes well together. Think about services that might go with your products.

1. By law, you must be able to supply what you intend to sell. If you want to sell dolls, keep well ahead of the demand or your business and reputation will be lost. You might even end up in a lawsuit.

If you're making dolls and state you will make them with either blond or brunette hair, have both done or have everything done but glueing on the wig. The idea that people appreciate an item more if they have to wait for it is untrue. You must be aware of federal postal regulations

CINDY McCLURE

Cindy McClure took time from her busy schedule to write her own story for me. I think you'll find it very interesting.

"Success in the doll world is a very individual endeavor. For me, my first success was to finish five dolls for Christmas, 1982; one for each of my five daughters. After this accomplishment, I pursued the idea of making my hobby a career. I set as my ultimate goal the design of original dolls and to have them made and distributed worldwide. Then I set a time schedule to follow, so I was always working toward a deadline. My original timetable for meeting this goal was 5 years, however, I was able to reach it within 2 years. This is how I did it:

1. Study. I purchased all of Mildred Seeley's workbooks and studied them, then chose one doll to reproduce first.

2. Buy one mold at a time. I worked on memorizing one doll at a time. I learned everything about her, including coloring, eyelashes, eyebrows, lips, cheeks, body types, dress styles, antique value and availability. Then I could reproduce the doll quickly and accurately.

3. Commit yourself. I signed up for a doll show a year in advance. This was the hardest step to take. I did my first doll show 5 months after taking my first doll class, which I would *never* advise anyone to do. I was still too new to really see how awful my work was. Nevertheless, I did two more shows after that and sold one doll—a $45 Googley. I realized people don't just buy any doll—they buy the *good* ones, no matter what the cost!

4. Analyze yourself. Take a break. Improve your skills. Be willing to work every day for months, if necessary. It took me 4 months to improve my painting. Then I did another doll show. Success was sweet, but for only a few hours. I sold 23 dolls only to have the money stolen from my car as I was leaving. Although devastated, the taste of success kept me going.

5. Enter competition. Be willing to take constructive criticism, and learn from it. Then try again.

6. Always keep your ultimate goal in mind. Even before my successful show, I began to sculpt. The idea for the fairies came from a sketch given to me by a friend. The face came from my baby, lying on my lap, fast asleep.

7. Advertise. Dress for success. Your dolls are worth more than jeans and a T-shirt. Make your display and yourself as much a work of art as your dolls are."

Cindy has now reached the height of a doll-artist's dream. Her 18 original dolls are being produced in Taiwan, in porcelain, completely under her supervision. Molds were made in Japan; materials, when necessary, came from China and the United States. Over 5,000 store accounts have already been opened across the United States. See full-page photo page 118.

about shipping items within a limited time.
2. It's better to have a mailing address listing a street address rather than a post-office box. Some people distrust post-office addresses, yet many successful businesses are run using only a box number. I know because I ran my plate business with a post-office box number.
3. It's difficult to talk about specific products, but there are some general things to be concerned about.
- Your product must be well-made and of high quality.
- It must be something people need or desire.
- It should be different, unusual and impossible or difficult to get elsewhere.
- Perhaps it is something new or a new idea.

4. A small item with a small price, if needed by almost every doll person, could make a small fortune for you. Paper goods or patterns are some of the best mail-order items because they don't deteriorate in storage, don't break in shipping, are easily packaged, cost little to produce and are inexpensive to ship.
5. Begin with a product you can stock in low quantities, then work up to meet demand. Reproduction dolls, old dolls and artist's dolls are probably the highest-priced, most popular items sold through the mail by doll people. Many people have found these businesses extremely successful.
6. Don't overlook the opportunity to add printed advertising or a new catalog in each package mailed out.
7. Your company name is *very* important! Don't use initials—it's confusing. Select an easily remembered name for your company that is short and connects with the products or services you are selling.
8. Guarantee your product. State this in your ads so customers know if they are not satisfied, they can return the item. This reassures potential customers.
9. Your product must be made or purchased at a price that will allow a reasonable profit on each sale. Keep your prices competitive, and be sure of your supply.
10. Add packing and postage charges to the price, or show packing and postage as an added cost. Usually the seller charges enough for packing and postage so it covers shipping to any state.
11. Project costs so you know something about how many units you have to sell to break even or make money. Figure in all your costs, such as postage, damaged products, products that can't be used, wrapping, workplace costs and the cost of the item.

PACKAGING

Packaging is important. A shipping package must be designed to stand up under conveyor belts and handling by carriers. It must arrive in relatively good condition. Be sure the item you sell fits the regulation sizes of the carrier. Check on insurance if you are shipping dolls.

Packing colorful or imaginative wrap adds to the interest of the product but may not bring you any extra profit. Be sure you have boxes, heavy paper, tape and printed labels ready before orders start to come in.

GETTING PAID

There are good ways to get paid for mail-order items—a check or money order with the order or sending the order C.O.D. (cash on delivery). It's difficult to collect the money after the item is shipped, and this is *not* advisable.

Many dolls are sold by time payments. I have always discouraged this. It's just as easy for the customer to put the money aside for a few months, then buy the doll. A purchase is less costly, and there is no chance the customer will lose her money when or if a payment is not made. As far as you're concerned, you are protected because you still have the product and some money. But it's a bad way to do business because customers may begin to dislike the payment and eventually the seller.

Take care of any complaints cheerfully. No matter how good your product is or how carefully made, some people will complain. Replace or adjust everything quickly and cheerfully, and make a refund if necessary. Some of your best repeat customers can be made this way.

Bonnie-Lee portrait dolls are sold exclusively through the mail. They are unique because each doll is modeled from a picture to represent someone. These are similar to the character dolls made many years ago. For more information on Bonnie-Lee portrait dolls, see the "Dollionaire" story on page 36.

OTHER CONSIDERATIONS

Bob Isbell was a great help to me in preparing a full-page advertisement for my mail-order plates. He had all the knowledge and art background to create just what I wanted. His color separations were great, and they reproduced beautifully in magazines. What sold the plates was their desirability, not my knowledge in creating the ad. In most instances, a good product, with good photos, will sell.

Mail-order business has ups and downs; some is seasonal. Business is usually good before Christmas and, surprisingly, during January and February. Summer months are not usually as good because people travel on vacations and may not be as interested in spending their money on dolls. Some fluctuation has to do with the place and page your ad was placed in a magazine.

You might try television; it's surprising how inexpensive some ads are. Inquiry should be followed up with direct mail of a brochure, catalog or other advertising. Television has not proven to be successful for most doll products, except for large productions like the Cabbage Patch Kids and other play dolls.

Once you have a customer, try to keep him with good, cheerful service. His repeat business is essential. Many repeat customers can make your business a thriving one.

Answer all the mail you receive from customers and potential customers. Personally sign all letters to give everything your "personal touch."

Ask customers for names and addresses of other interested doll people. Ask for names of friends, relatives, neighbors or others in their doll club who might be interested in receiving information about your product. Follow this up by sending your catalog or brochure.

THE CATALOG OR BROCHURE

The vehicle of success in many mail-order businesses is the catalog or brochure. For many mail-order companies, this piece of literature is the *only* salesman you have to sell your product. It is the only contact between the public and your doll business. Catalogs and brochures come in all forms and sizes—from a few sheets stapled together to elaborate, full-color catalogs of the successful doll companies.

Good catalogs are like good salesmen. One of the most important things for a mail-order business is an attractive, orderly catalog.

A catalog is important, and its quality is important. Your reputation and work are represented on the pages the buyer will see. People know you only by the catalog or brochure you produce.

Effective catalogs and brochures can be many types, and they can do dramatic things for your business—or they can be completely ignored and thrown into the garbage with junk mail. If you plan to sell by catalog and brochure, consider how the receiver will feel when she reads yours.

Catalogs—Catalogs are expensive to produce, and some larger companies put a price on theirs. Repeat customers receive their catalogs free. Some businesses deduct the price of the catalog from the first order; others do not. Some companies sell their catalogs through small magazine ads.

A catalog, whether small or large, must have character. It must appeal to the doll lover and have enough items or items of great enough value to make it pay to produce and mail the catalog.

In the early days of our business, I made doll-mold catalogs by cutting up black and white photos that I had taken. I pasted the pictures, along with a number, a description and price, on a sheet. I took this to a photo offset printer, along with a design for the cover, an order blank and instructions for ordering. All this was done in black and white.

Our catalogs grew with our business. When we began, there was little competition in the doll world, so our catalogs didn't have to be that great. I had to learn by doing because there were no other doll-mold catalogs at that time.

Today, color is what sells the items in many catalogs. You must present the item or doll in the best possible light. It almost has to be a dramatic presentation. If it's a picture of a doll, it must have so much appeal that the doll is irresistible. Smaller items can be presented in small black-and-white photos.

When you put your catalog together, use a good printer. Use every bit of space for advertising because you must pay postage.

There are two ways that you can prepare a catalog when you begin. Start with a sharp, dramatic, expensive catalog in the beginning and take a chance on its being very successful. Or start with a homemade, inexpensive catalog produced in a copy shop. This could get you started with very little capital outlay.

Remember—the catalog is your salesman—it represents you and your products.

PRESCOTT CASE CO.

The Prescott Case Co. makes glass cases for dolls and other special treasures. Mathew Files and eight others started the community business 10 years ago. Today, 30 people are involved in it. Besides making glass cases, the company makes stained glass, does weaving and has a printing operation. They have over 400 accounts for cases. Most of the group are college graduates. Files attributes the group's success to giving prompt, reliable service and their dedication to the community.

CHARLOTTE BYRD

Charlotte V. Byrd, an original-doll artist, makes historical portrait dolls in limited editions. Each porcelain doll is signed and numbered, and every modeling detail is done to perfection. Most of Charlotte's dolls have wired cloth bodies and are costumed carefully with every detail correct. Perfection has been her password to success.

NANCY AND JIM BLAIR

The Blairs have done it! They have mechanized three types of full-sized doll bodies—a large German doll body, a toddler body and a Baby Hilda body. The dolls do many things, such as play the violin, play with blocks or almost anything you can think of. Nancy and Jim sell the bodies ready to work, and you make the head and dress the doll. The Blairs are just discovering what a little ingenuity and hard work can do!

If you're interested in buying one of these bodies, check out the supplier list on page 123.

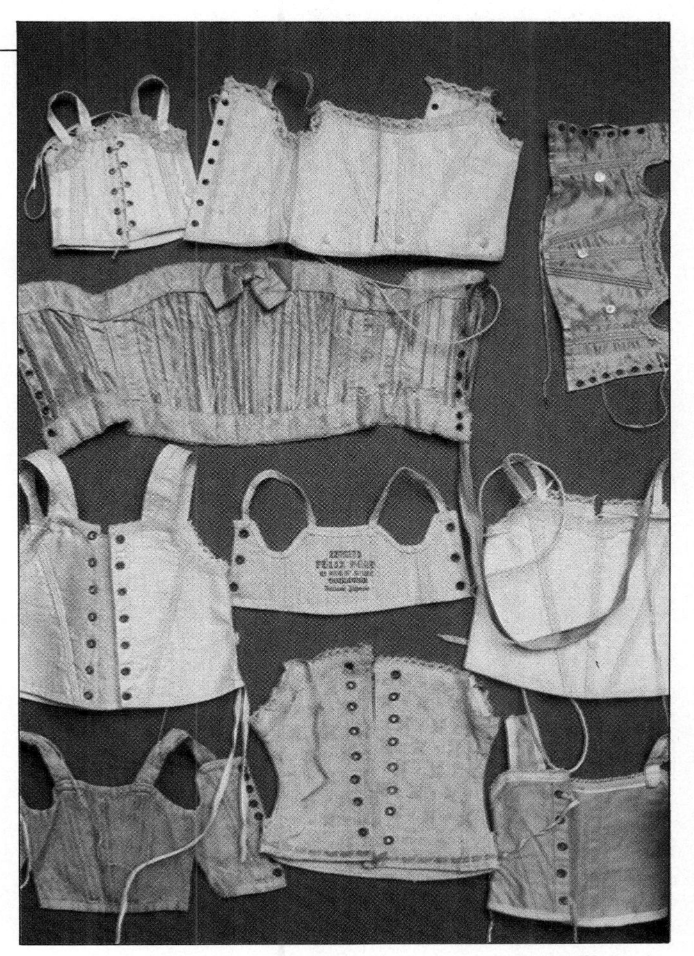

Corsets from Mickie's and Sandy's Antique Dolls in Phoenix, Arizona. Many accessories for dolls, along with other doll-related items, can be found in catalogs.

Your Doll Studio

There are only a few of what I consider "perfect" doll studios (places where people can make dolls) in existence today—most people have to make do with the space and facilities they have available. But sometimes there are things you can do to improve the facility you do have. The following ideas can apply to any studio—whether classes are held there or not.

WORK SPACE

The most important thing for a doll studio is adequate space to work. Don't crowd in extra students to fill every nook and cranny. Figure out how much space you have, and don't take more students than you have sufficient work space for.

Many studios are messy, and students have to clean off a place to work before they can begin. Provide tables with essentials on them, and make your studio clean and cheerful. This is important so students feel good about their surroundings.

LIGHT

You need enough light for each work space. Over the years, I have found good overhead lighting can be provided by fluorescent tubes, and it provides the best overall lighting. If you do not have enough lights, add them to the workroom *before* you start classes. There is nothing that turns a student away from studio work faster than poor lighting.

EXAMPLES OF DOLLS

By having a few perfect examples of finished dolls in the studio, you provide an example and an inspiration for your students. With a perfect example, you immediately gain the admiration of your students. They will look up to you, listen to what you have to say and aim for perfection, either consciously or unconsciously.

Left: Hat making is an art. Jackie Jones uses skills she learned as a Chicago hat maker many years ago to make doll hats. Doll in front is E.J., in back P.D.

Mary K. Stevens teaching a class in one of her two studios. She is a three-time Millie winner. See "Dollionaire" story about Mary on the opposite page.

I don't believe all beginning teachers must be able to produce perfect dolls, but they must know the methods for making dolls. I believe a new teacher must be honest with her students and tell them she has not yet perfected a part of doll making, such as painting eyebrows for French dolls.

But the teacher must show a photo of an antique doll or a doll from another teacher that demonstrates perfect painting. A teacher must not allow students to copy anything that is less than perfect. If you've ever seen a reproduction doll done from another reproduction doll, you know what I mean. Go back to the original antique doll, a photograph of the old doll or a perfect reproduction. Don't set an example that will let your studio depreciate into making junk.

STUDIO COMFORT

A studio must have adequate warmth and air conditioning; students must be comfortable. As the teacher, you must be conscious of your student's continued comfort.

Chairs that people will sit in for 2 or more hours must be comfortable. Makeshift chairs of varying heights are not good. In one studio I visited, people were coming in a half hour before class time—to get the best chairs!

WATER

A studio must have water available, with a sink in the teaching room. Be sure there is a bathroom, and keep it clean. Some studios provide coffee or a small snack to give students a break. It's also nice for your students if you have a drinking fountain for their use.

THE KILN

Don't place your kiln in the teaching room. If it must be located in the teaching room, don't fire it while classes are in session. A kiln gives off toxic fumes and can be uncomfortable to sit close to because of the heat. Adequate ventilation must be available. For instance, if you're doing gold firings, your class may leave because of the odor. Other firing is not as bad, but there is some odor and too much heat. Keep your students in mind, and think of their comfort.

THE STUDIO AS AN INSPIRATION

Let your studio be an inspiration to all who enter. Use charts, posters and models that fit a particular lesson. But don't allow a student to get ahead of herself by putting up charts or showing models for the third lesson before she has the second lesson.

MARY K. STEVENS

Mary K. Stevens began making doll clothes for doll-making teachers and doll collectors in January 1980. She became intrigued with the lovely porcelain dolls and traded doll clothes for classes. In November 1980, she completed her first doll. Since 1980, she has made her mark in the doll world by winning three Millie awards in 14 months!

In 1981, she joined the Doll Artisan Guild. She began teaching classes in the basement of her home in northern Illinois. She soon outgrew that facility and began a succession of moves to larger shops. By September 1985, it was necessary to open a second shop, which is run by her daughter, Cindy.

Mary has over 80 regular pupils in her classes, and some of her students travel more than 40 miles (each way) to attend weekly sessions. She is an excellent teacher—she shares her techniques, important information and "doll" trivia as she mingles with her students. Her cheerful, patient manner has earned her the love and respect of her "doll ladies." The quality of her teaching is evident in the work of her students; three have won Millie awards. Her local seminars attract people from several neighboring states, and when she conducts seminars on the road, she is very well-received.

Mary's success as an artisan is unique, and her success as a businesswoman is enviable. Mary was born and raised in Belhaven, North Carolina, left high school and married at 17, had three children, raised three foster children, had no formal art training and was not exposed to porcelain dolls until 1980. Mary attributes her success to the support, encouragement and help of her family and the grace of God. But those of us who know her understand her success comes from hard work, dedication, love of beauty and a desire to preserve history. She is an inspiration to all who know her. Written by Phyllis Babbs, one of Mary's students.

EVALUATE YOUR STUDIO

Take a look at the points we have covered. How does your studio rate? Are you making a good income? Maybe there are areas for improvement in the physical side of the studio, the operation part, the teaching part or advertising. If you can figure out what you can do better and do it, your bank account will reflect it.

RUNNING A SUCCESSFUL STUDIO

The techniques covered below are some I have discovered for running a doll studio. These ideas apply to any kind of doll making.

Running a studio is no game. A good studio is a profit-making venture. Never apologize for charging your students a price by which you, the studio operator, can get ahead.

When you name your studio, or rename it, choose something with the word *doll* in the title or, better still, doll and location in title. If your studio has been a ceramic studio and now you concentrate on dolls, rename it. It will help your business. People will be aware that it is now a doll studio.

Adequate parking is essential. If you have a problem with parking, try to make arrangements with a neighboring business to use their parking space. You might ask about using a private driveway, and rent the space for certain times. In addition to parking, adequate outside lighting is necessary for safety's sake if you offer night classes.

If you're setting up a studio and looking for a place to rent, check inside facilities and look at the neighborhood. Don't put a doll studio in an area that people will not feel safe or a place that is too out of the way. Post signs in windows or use decorations that indicate dolls. New students may come in when they see them.

THE STUDIO TEACHER

A teacher-studio operator is like a mother who is all things to her children—cook, chauffeur, nurse, adviser. The list is unending and forever changing for a teacher-studio operator. You are expected to be a skillful painter of dolls, a costumer, a wig maker, perhaps even a shoemaker. And this is only the beginning.

You're supposed to be a good demonstrator and a patient teacher. You need to be a financial wizard at running a studio to make it profitable, an engineer to operate the kiln, a janitor to keep it clean and a "strong man" for pouring and stacking molds.

In addition to these skills, you need to be able to bring everything together, be ready when the students are and make it all appear as if there was nothing to it.

Most teachers begin by doing everything themselves because this is the way to get started. In a short time, it's easy to see if the operation is going to be a success. If there are more people wanting classes than you can get in and if the dolls are coming out good and students are happy, you have a chance at success.

A great teacher must separate herself from the "regular work" and give more classes and devote more time to teaching. Assign clean-up work and odd jobs to another person. Teach another person to pour molds, fire and do things so you can save your time, which is better paid for teaching.

There are many kinds of arrangements for teaching. Some teachers prefer to teach for a salary or a percentage in someone else's studio, leaving the studio work to the owner. Some studio owners can't teach so they prefer a teacher that will come in to teach classes for them.

If you think you want to teach doll making, below is a list of things to consider *before* you make your decision. They must all be combined with the ability to teach.

A good doll-making teacher:

- Must be unselfish; she must think first of her students.
- Must impart to her students all she knows and tell them where to find what she doesn't know.
- Is more interested in her reputation as a fine teacher than she is in selling her finished dolls.
- Receives more thrills from seeing her students get an award for a doll than she would from getting it herself.
- Can view a student's broken greenware head with a smile and say, "I have another one for you." (When a new student breaks a head, it can seem like a major disaster.)
- Studies her class and discovers the capabilities of each student. She knows how far she can expect each to progress and drives them only to *that* point of perfection.
- Is friendly and understanding.
- Looks out for the physical comfort of her class. She keeps the room warm or cool and moves someone if they are not compatible or are too neighborly. She attempts to provide just the right atmosphere for work.

PRIVATE LESSONS

Private lessons in doll making are handled a little differently than class work. Private lessons command a much higher price if you, as the teacher, are an expert. The length of a lesson is shorter; the number of lessons and when they are held are often determined by the student's and teacher's schedules.

The price of a private lesson may or may not include the price of the materials to make a doll. Private students work at their own pace and usually advance much faster than students in classes. Giving private lessons is a good way to start if you intend to become a teacher.

There is another angle to private lessons that you must consider. If you're the timid type and are unsure if you can handle teaching but would like the added income, give some private lessons. Tell your student in the beginning you have not taught before, and charge accordingly.

If you're a "kitchen doll maker," with almost no room to work, you can still give private lessons, especially if your dolls are superior. Share your knowledge, and your students will be forever grateful. We must all start somewhere.

There are some great teachers in different parts of the country. If you feel you have gone as far as you can go by yourself or with a local studio, try to get a seminar or a few private lessons from one of these great teachers. These teachers are all very human, and a telephone call will probably get you a few lessons. Sometimes you can learn more from one of these people in a day or two than you can get in months elsewhere. Make up the extra money you spend in travel and lessons by teaching others and demanding a better price for each lesson. In the doll world, knowledge and skill make money. Contact the Doll Artisan Guild for a seminar schedule or a list of teachers.

Some studios have "private lessons," but it's really what I call an *open studio*. The studio is open for students to come in and make dolls. Each student does her own thing in her own time on the doll of her choice. The teacher spends a little time with each student or helps them as needed. Some teachers and some students like this method. The student usually pays for studio time, doll parts, firing and any other costs incurred.

In a doll business, you can do your own thing and make whatever pleases you, such as this type of doll.

THE STUDENT-TEACHER

In many cases, an assistant is necessary in the doll classroom. One studio I know of tested an old idea—they used a student-teacher, also called an *apprentice*. She was a good student from one class and wished to learn more about teaching. The student-teacher worked for a certain length of time for the chance to learn, not for money. In exchange she was allowed to take seminars, fire her doll heads along with the class and use the instructor's library and patterns.

In this case, the student-teacher soon became good enough to handle a children's class and a beginner's class. At the end of her apprenticeship, she had the choice to set up her own studio or work for her teacher. She chose not to have the headaches of buying kilns, paying rent and doing advertising, so she stayed with her teacher for a salary. The situation has worked out with great satisfaction for both.

This is an idea worth trying in your studio. Choose the student wisely, don't make the apprenticeship too long and give her lots of responsibility. If she decides to go off and set up a studio, select another student as an apprentice. Sometimes, a teenage son or daughter will like this arrangement.

Mechanical doll at the Oakland Doll Show, 1985. The base and mechanism were purchased, and the doll was built and dressed around it. Teaching about making mechanicals could be a good subject area to consider.

DEMONSTRATIONS

From a recent survey I took, I found most teachers and many seminar teachers cannot, or do not, give satisfactory demonstrations. Some of the demonstrations are poorly prepared, and some teachers even fail to give prepared demonstrations. Anyone skilled in teaching and teaching techniques knows a good demonstration is the key to teaching good doll-making techniques.

A *good* demonstration teaches by showing a method, a technique or the best way to get desired results. A good demonstration also shows desired results. Demonstrating is the quickest, most satisfactory way to teach a group to do something.

To prepare and give a good demonstration:

1. Make a list of materials needed.
2. List procedures in chronological order.
3. Test your planned demonstration several times.
4. Have a completely finished product to show at the end of your demonstration.
5. Summarize the steps.

Make charts, use a blackboard or hand out a sheet with important facts listed on it. You might include:

- Materials needed (if necessary where they can be purchased).
- Steps in the procedure and tools, such as brushes and oils, where appropriate.
- Definition of unusual or new terms used in the demonstration; use drawings when necessary.
- Summary of the demonstration.

Below is a step-by-step guide to help you prepare and give the best demonstration possible. Follow these steps to help you prepare to give your next demonstration.

Step 1. Give the demonstration in a planned, orderly fashion. Take only the time that is necessary. Be straightforward, and use short, clearly understood sentences. Know *exactly* what you're doing and what results you'll get. Use only methods you have tested. If you use this method of giving demonstrations, you'll probably be very successful at it.

Step 2. Gather together all the equipment and materials you're going to use, and put them on a tray. When possible, place things you use in order of the first-used nearest you. After using the tool, place it on another tray.

Step 3. Have a completely finished product to show at the end of your demonstration, but keep it covered so it won't be seen until you're finished. Otherwise, students will be looking at it instead of following your demonstration.

Step 4. Before you start, read or give everyone a list of materials needed so your audience is familiar with the items, such as types of brushes, size numbers of brushes, sizes of pen points, grit sizes on scrubbers.

Step 5. Give the demonstration in steps, and give the reasons for each step. Show results of each step and a completely finished product.

Step 6. Summarize by listing materials and reading the steps again. Leave nothing to the imagination. Perhaps you have watched in awe as Julia Child demonstrated her cooking techniques. Notice how she pulls the finished product from the oven to put the crowning touch on her demonstration. You can do the same!

Step 7. When you're teaching or demonstrating doll making, teach what you consider the best method. Don't confuse students by teaching and showing several methods of doing the same thing; you'll end up with students doing a mixture, resulting in poor work. Some people do things one way, some do it another and everyone gets the same good results. Be open-minded about methods, but teach "your" way. When you summarize, describe other methods, and tell students where they can find information on them. Let them know you are aware of other procedures that are as good as yours.

Step 8. Be sure all the steps are discussed and all the materials you use are included. When people first started teaching about doll making, their hearts were not in it. They secretly wanted to keep the things they had learned to themselves. At one demonstration I saw, a teacher left out an important step so the students would not come out with dolls as good as hers. Another teacher left out the step of sanding the bisque before painting—on purpose! A third left out oiling bisque before applying cheek blush!

Step 9. When preparing to give a demonstration, be sure everyone watches you. Don't allow students to work, clean up or prepare anything while you're demonstrating. Demand their undivided attention. Ask them to hold questions during your demonstration, and tell them you'll answer all their questions when you have finished.

Step 10. The arrangement of tables and seating can make your demonstration successful or unsuccessful. If your students can't see or hear everything, the demonstration has not fulfilled its purpose. I like chairs arranged around tables on the outside of a horseshoe shape for demonstrating.

Step 11. Never stand in front of strong light, such as a sunny window, when demonstrating. It's too hard on students' eyes.

Step 12. Be sure students can see all the procedures; anything small should be shown on an an enlarged model or chart. For instance, when demonstrating how to paint eyelashes, use the largest head you can find, and also show how it's done with a chart or large drawing.

Good demonstrations will increase your skill as a teacher, and your students will have better results. It will allow you to have larger classes, and your students will progress more quickly.

There's a big difference between knowing something or being able to do something and being able to teach it or demonstrate it. Being a top demonstrator will earn you a reputation as a teacher and bring in more students, who will be willing to pay more for a good teacher.

VIDA WEST

Vida Florante West developed her own unique method of making implanted-hair doll wigs. She makes her own wig bases and calls them *vida cups*. She also makes special tools for wig makers. Vida makes special wigs for dolls and shares her knowledge and skill with all who want to learn through her illustrated articles and seminars. Sharing makes the difference to Vida.

SIMULATED DEMONSTRATIONS

There are many procedures in making a doll that should be shown with a simulated demonstration or reshown with a fake demonstration. A simulated demonstration is a method of demonstrating a technique without actually using some of the materials. For example, there are some simple things, such as the motion of the brush in applying cheek blush, that can be demonstrated several times with a *dry* brush so the student gets the idea of how to do it. The student will do a better job the first time if she works first with a dry brush to get the idea of motion. Even eyelashes can be demonstrated with a dry brush to show how to apply them.

Many simulated demonstrations show a process that is too long or too complicated or there is a chance that something will go wrong. One thing I have always liked to show with a simulated demonstration is how to set sleep eyes. The process is best shown with half a fired head with sleep eyes already set in it. Students can work the eyes, see how they should fit and see where and how plaster is applied. Then I give the steps in setting the eyes.

If students are to be teachers, I go through the process of making a half-head, then tell and show how the eyes are set. This is important for them to know so they can make a model that can be used for teaching how to set sleep eyes for their students.

A similar model can be used for teaching how to set paperweight eyes. The half-head model is used because it is impossible to see down into a doll head to show how each step is carried out and how the finished eyes will look and work.

In demonstrating the perfection needed to make eyebrows for French dolls, a simulated demonstration is often better than an actual demonstration using paint, especially if you're nervous or afraid you'll come out with less-than-perfect eyebrows if you use paint. A doll head that has been fired is better to pass around for students to examine—it will go around the class in perfect condition. A freshly painted head may get smudged accidentally before everyone has examined it closely.

In many instances, a chart or enlarged drawing will show a process better than a demonstration. For instance, an enlarged drawing of stringing a doll is clearer than actually stringing a small doll. A drawing will show many things, such as the shape of the head and the pieces that go into the neck—the glove leather, the neck button and wire hook. It can show how body elastic is hooked. On a separate chart, you can show how a shoulder head is strung. This avoids confusion, and the drawing imprints on a student's mind better than a pile of hooks and buttons being dropped into a doll. To give the best demonstration possible, do the actual stringing, and use the charts for extra emphasis.

Charts, models and half-done dolls are important to a studio teacher or seminar teacher—I cannot put enough emphasis on this. They are important tools for teaching.

I must point out that the teacher who does a better job of teaching and demonstrating is the teacher who lasts. She is the teacher with students lined up weeks ahead, waiting for a class. She is also the teacher with the greatest income.

CONTROLLING THE CLASS

At the beginning of a class, you must make it clear to the participants that all their questions will be answered but not during a demonstration. Ask them to write down their question, and if it has not been answered before you finish the lecture, you will answer any questions at the end.

There are several reasons for handling your class this way. There will always be one or two individuals who will dominate the class, and they will try to monopolize your teaching time with their questions. This must be taken care of at the *very beginning* of the class. All students are equal and must get equal time.

Another reason for having questions at the end is that many questions will be answered in *proper sequence* during your lecture. To answer questions as the students think them up throws the whole sequence off and may disrupt your demonstration.

As the teacher, you must have complete control of the lecture, demonstration, student questions and conversation. Class control is important. Expect everyone to be looking at you and paying attention when you're lecturing. At this point in their learning, think of students as children; don't hesitate to ask for their undivided attention. It will save time for all, and you won't have to repeat many things. Tell your students this is the way you conduct the class, and ask for their cooperation. Treat them like adults who are participating in the class for their own enjoyment—you'll get more cooperation if you're firm and let them know what to expect.

Ask for a studio atmosphere when people are working. Some people are sensitive to loud talking and can't concentrate with people visiting back and forth. Many people are sensitive to smoke, so if people must smoke, ask them to go outside. Give a break time for essentials. Suggest students stretch and walk around to give their muscles and eyes a rest.

You may want to plan something special for break time, such as looking at an exhibit in another room, viewing slides or offering something to eat or drink. *Don't* let students eat and work at the same time. There are too many toxic substances in china paints and dust in greenware—there could be problems if these are ingested.

It's up to you to help students develop good work habits. Try to establish a relaxed, easy-going, you-can-do-it atmosphere. Keep an eye on each student, and make sure no one is being annoyed by talking neighbors. If this happens, give the student the opportunity to move.

REPRODUCTION DOLLMAKING CLASSES

Advanced registration required.
Class size will be limited to 8 students.
Student fee: $5.00 per class session.
Instructions will cover:
a. Cleaning of greenware.
b. Use of tools.
c. China painting techniques as applies to dollmaking.
All supplies, necessary for these instructions, will be provided for the students use durring the class session.

Seperate costs will be:
a. Greenware
b. Firing
c. Eyes
d. Wigs
e. Stringing materials
f. Patterns
Greenware replacement parts will be provided free of charge on first doll only. Subsequent breakage will be replaced at cost.

Greenware purchased elsewhere is not an acceptable class project and should not be brought into the studio while classes are in session. Use of the studio for a $2.50 fee is available at any time there is no scheduled class and these dolls may be cleaned and painted at this time. A seperate price sheet is posted for firing these dolls.

Library

My private library is available to any student wishing to research the doll being reproduced. These books may not be removed from the studio.

Doll classes are advertised in newspapers, on bulletins boards and at studios. Study this class announcement; it's a good example and includes all the necessary information.

CLASSROOM JUDGING

At the end of a series of lessons on any kind of doll making, pretend you're having a doll show; students will be the judges. Give them a judging sheet, and explain how it is used. The classroom teacher can make up a sheet giving a number of points for each part of the doll made. In an advanced class, students can use a judging sheet from a Doll Artisan Guild doll show. Explain how to use the judging sheet, and let students judge each other's work.

Get the students talking about good and bad doll painting. Teach them to criticize their work and to be criticized without being hurt. This brings the doll-making process to life so students can see what judges will see (and what they—the students—haven't seen) at a real doll show.

Classroom judging can be a fun project and a good learning tool. But it must be done very carefully so no feels hurt and everyone is happy.

DOLL-CLASS ADVERTISING

To enroll more people in your doll classes and to be able to offer more classes, you must advertise. Advertise in as many ways as you can so everyone who might take a class knows about the classes you offer. I have included some examples on the following pages.

Some advertising takes money, some takes ambition and some takes a creative mind. Use all three—money, ambition and creativity—for best results.

Have notices printed on bright paper or with brightly colored ink, and distribute them to places where there is a public bulletin board, such as grocery stores and laundromats. Ask anyone who has a doll store to put them on their counter. Put flyers on the free table at doll shows in your area. Put your announcements in antique, toy or home shows. Put the notice in teacher bulletins. Do you have a friend in a doll club, women's club or garden club who might announce your classes for you? Post notices in your studio or store window. Perhaps your local newspaper would like to do an article on you and your studio—it could end with class announcements.

Exhibits always attract attention, so put exhibits that call attention to your fine work in a bank, the library, a retirement center or a store window. Along with the exhibit, include an announcement of your classes. Put up exhibits at fairs and local functions, such as craft shows or art shows, that allow you to do so.

Offer to give a demonstration, such as at a shopping mall, a church, a 4-H meeting, for scout troops, Agricultural Extension programs or a street fair. This is not easy, but people will learn about you and your studio, and this may create a desire in others to make dolls.

Arrange for class times to be convenient for prospective doll makers. Plan on making dolls that will appeal to your prospective students. Try some doll-making classes for children in the afternoon or on a Saturday morning. Sometimes this can be done for a club, such as 4-H or the scouts.

Hold classes for teachers on Friday evenings. Classes with a special rate for senior citizens in the morning are often filled. Doll classes for mothers or homemakers held in the morning or early afternoon, before children get home from school, are often very popular. Consider holding doll classes for working people on a Saturday or Sunday morning and include brunch.

JEAN KINCAID

Jean Kincaid sandwiches her doll success with reproduction dolls between a full-time job, two doll clubs and community and church work. After 25 years in ceramics, she tried one doll and never did any more ceramics. Success to Jean is her happiness in her lovely creations.

When setting up classes, think of your students—when can they come, what will get them to come, what will keep them coming?

Costs of Advertising—Advertising your shop and classes usually costs money. Money spent on advertising should come back doubled. Business cannot come to your door unless people know the door is there and what is beyond it. Newspaper advertising gets the quickest results.

You might try one of the eye-catching phrases listed below. Follow the headline with complete information concerning classes that you will be holding. Ads don't need to be large, but they must be eye-catching. Try creating different headlines.

- Experience Doll Making
- Experience the Joys of Doll Making
- Make Your Own Doll—Classes Starting
- Special French-Doll Classes—for Advanced Students
- Begin Now—Be a Doll Artist—Begin Now
- It's Never Too Late to Be a Doll Artist!

- Be a Professional Doll Artist
- Learn Doll Making for Fun
- Have the Time of Your Life—Make A Doll
- Be Creative—Make Dolls
- Do What You've Always Wanted—Make Dolls
- Make a Doll at My House—Private Lessons, Choose Your Doll

Follow your eye-catching headline with information about the class, such as the examples shown below:

> Experience Doll Making—Beginner's classes starting June 1, from 9 a.m. to 11:30 a.m., Tuesday and Friday. Series of six organized lessons and demonstrations. Will completely finish two bisque dolls. Call 555-1234 for information between 9 a.m. and 5 p.m., or stop at Second Childhood Dolls, 925 E. Doll Avenue.

> Special Advanced Doll-Making Classes starting April 28. Classes from 1:30 to 4:30 p.m., Wednesday and Friday for 4 consecutive weeks. Will complete three dolls—Long-Faced Jumeau, Stobé and A.T. Start from greenware. Instructor certified in making French dolls. Call 555-4567 for further information. Other classes evenings and Saturday mornings. Doll One Studio, 321 Jumeau St.

> The Joys of Doll Making—Felt dolls taught in air-conditioned studio from 9 a.m. to 12 p.m. or 1 p.m. to 4 p.m. Pick your time. Individual instruction. Choose your doll. Call 555-1000 any time. All types of dolls taught. Old Time Dolls, 156 N. Porcelain Ave.

It's good to have special, nationally known instructors come in to the studio several times a year to hold seminars. These classes and demonstrations are expensive for students, and you don't make much on them, but they are usually worth it. They give you a chance to advertise and get people to your studio. You'll always have people who think someone from the outside world can do a better job and will come for the seminar.

Salien Jones with two of her Personettes, or Stars in Miniature. These are very large, very lifelike dolls that Salien has made. Exhibiting original dolls may help increase interest in doll-making classes.

At the end of a series of classes, have an open house or exhibit the dolls students made in some public place. Use any publicity the show generates to sign up new students.

CREATING INTEREST IN DOLL MAKING

An interest in dolls can be found in many men and women; it only has to be brought to the surface. There are many ways to create an interest in dolls, but they all require time to prepare—some take more time than others. Try the following ideas to help create interest in your doll-making programs.

Set up an exhibit of finished dolls in your local library, along with workbooks and your studio address and telephone number. Show a couple of reproduction dolls and a photo of the original antique doll.

Hold an exhibit at a bank, restaurant, airport, hospital or retirement center. Examine your community for any possible place for a doll display. Never leave an exhibit in a place long enough for it to get faded or discolored. Be sure exhibits in your studio are the best you can make them.

Any place you can give a short demonstration will help advertise your talent and your classes. Craft shows, antique shows and other community events are good places to demonstrate doll making or show dolls.

Doll Shows—An even better way to generate interest in dolls is to hold a doll show. Even small communities put on shows in connection with a historical society, library, department store, house tour or other community event. Doll shows almost run themselves.

Involve as many doll studios and doll dealers as possible. It should be a combination of old dolls, doll items and reproduction dolls for sale. These occasions should include doll demonstrations and places to sign up for classes. Occasionally miniature dolls and doll houses are added to the show.

If you're thinking of organizing a doll show, advertising will be your most important undertaking. Have posters printed, and put them in grocery stores, laundries, public buildings and any place else you can think of. Place advertisements in local newspapers, and mail notices to friends of the studio and anyone else who might be interested.

If you can get on television, it will help create interest in dolls and doll making. TV seems to reach the largest audience in the shortest amount of time. Sometimes public-service announcements (PSAs) on television are set aside for local meetings. Occasionally, when a local channel knows about your dolls, they'll find a spot for you on a community program.

You must have top dolls to show on television. Expect instant results, such as telephone calls. For some doll-show television interviews, studios try to get a doll celebrity, a well-known teacher, a collector or a writer to speak for them on the show. Often shows will have a special guest as an added attraction. This sometimes adds just the right touch to expand interest in doll making.

Doll and Teddy Bear Show and Sale June 2, 3, 1984

Wayne, Pennsylvania
Free Admission
11am-4pm

Come and meet manufacturers representatives who will answer your questions. See the beautiful dolls and teddy bears on display, many with special show prices. Featuring: Effanbee, Suzanne Gibson, Royal Dolls, Dolls by Pauline, Sasha, Heidi Ott, Stupsi, Crolle, Kewpie, Zapf, Gund, North American Bear, and Steiff including limited edition sets.

See you at the show!

Above and right: Doll shows have become common after 10 years. Before this, shows were not open to the public, and very few were held. Doll-show advertising must be done carefully.

THE SEMINAR TEACHER

A *seminar* is a short, intensive course taught by an expert. Usually, but not always, a *seminar teacher* is employed by a company to advertise their products—the company pays her travel expenses and pays her for teaching because she uses their products. A company has access to studios and their customers all over the country and can advertise very well.

A seminar teacher must be special to be successful. She must be an expert in *every* phase of doll making she teaches. This is the most important criteria for a seminar teacher. She must be able to *teach* someone how to make a doll, to get others to do what she does and come out with excellent results. She must be a top demonstrator.

A seminar teacher must know what she needs for each lesson and carry it with her or be sure it will be provided. She must always carry fine examples of her work with her on the road.

A good instructor needs to be familiar with old dolls—their painting, history and original

THE RUEGERS

The Ruegers are friendly people, and they specialize in clowns. They use commercial molds of antique dolls and make them into delightful clowns. They made the Marque mold into a mechanical clown doll, with music. The Ruegers attend trade shows and sell dolls in major showrooms all over the West Coast. Julia says they take great pride in their dolls and try to keep the quality of finished products high. Besides good marketing and their perfection in workmanship, the novel idea of making only clowns has made them "Dollionaires."

costumes. She must have an appreciation for the art of doll making.

The seminar teacher must be able to leave her home and family for weeks at a time. She must be able to plan ahead so she has everything with her. She must be independent because she cannot depend on others if plans are changed or classes cancelled. She must adjust and feel at home in hotels, motels or private homes—wherever she is housed.

This special teacher must be able to work in any kind of studio, with crowded conditions or poor lighting, with whatever tools are available. She must make friends easily and be able to gain the respect of her students. She must be able to build the confidence of those in her classes. These things are a natural part of the teaching personality of a seminar teacher.

The seminar teacher must keep her presentation on the subject of dolls and keep personal problems to herself. She must *never* talk about other teachers. These are two of the biggest complaints I hear about seminar teachers—time spent on personal problems and talking about other teachers!

The nicest arrangement is one in which a husband and wife travel and teach together—they can enjoy the trip and help each other with their work. Retired couples make excellent seminar teachers.

Some teachers are not loyal to the company that pays them—in a seminar they use or mention products from other companies. This *will* get back to the company. If you're being paid to teach by a company and you accept this position, you must be loyal to that company. If you don't like the company, don't teach for them!

Seminars must be planned months in advance. Usually they are planned so a teacher can go from one to the other without great travel expense, such as being in California and doing several seminars in the same area. This is one reason many seminars are set up by companies. They have the distributors and the advertising to make the trip time productive.

To All Doll Enthusiasts:

This is an invitation to the

THIRD SOUTHEASTERN DOLL SYMPOSIUM

June 5-8, 1985

to be held on the beautiful campus of

Meredith College, Raleigh, North Carolina

(co-sponsored by the College and the Sir Walter Raleigh Doll Club)

For information, write or call
Office of Alumnae Affairs
Meredith College
Raleigh, North Carolina 27607-5298
(919) 833-6461

Above and right: Putting on doll seminars and symposiums is a new business in itself. These announcements show what types of information to include in your flyer.

Gini Wisner

Doll Seminars NW

Division of Little People

November 9, 1985 is the beginning of a unique experience . . .

A series of one day seminars taught by leading Northwest Dealers and Collectors with Special National Guest Lecturers . . . . . .

ACTUAL VIEWING EXPERIENCE   OUTLINES PROVIDED   QUESTIONS ANSWERED
SOURCES   NEWSBRIEF: AMISH DOLLS

SPEAKERS

YVONNE BAIRD — One of the Northwest's leading doll dealers from Olympia; Sponsor NW Doll & Toy Mart; Yvonne left a lucrative professional career to dedicate her knowledge and talent to the Doll World.

HAZEL COONS — Well-known for her in-depth knowledge and life long love affair with the French Bebes; Travelled throughout Europe and the U.S.; Insatiable pursuit of knowledge and collecting.

BEV PORT — For 25 years a noted international Teddy Bear & Doll Artist, Author, & Lecturer; Creator of Time Machine Teddies; From Bremerton, Bev writes for *Doll Reader, Teddy Bears & Friends, Doll Value Quarterly;* appears on TV around the country; Member Original Doll Artist Council of America; Founding member American Bear Artist Guild; International Doll Academy; UFDC (National Board 79-81); Good Bears of the World; National Association of Miniature Enthusiasts.

JUDY ROBERTS — From Spokane; Owner of over 400 Barbies; Member International Barbie Doll Collectors Club; International Barbie Doll Collectors; Member Inland Empire Doll Club; 10 years of study and collection and attendance at national seminars.

JULIE SCOTT — "Plumed Horse"; Owner of Two Mall Shops: Heritage in Kirkland and Days Gone Bye in Redmond; Regular exhibitor NW Doll & Toy Mart; Juanita Antique Exp.; President of Lake East Doll Club; Julie specializes in carousel and hobby horses, dolls, toys and children's items.

RICHARD WRIGHT — Our National Speaker hails from Connecticut; experienced in the antique world since he was 11 thru his Mother, Beatrice Wright; Owner of Antique Shop; Known throughout the Doll World for his extensive collection of antique and early dolls; examples appear in almost every book on Antique Dolls including THE BLUE BOOK; Appeared on TV; Series of articles for Collector's Showcase; Travels world-wide for pristine examples; regular exhibitor at many U.S. shows; We are proud to have Richard take time from his busy schedule to share his knowledge with us.

921 Sunset Way, Bellevue, WA 98004 (206) 454-9635

SUGGESTIONS FOR CLASSES AND TEACHERS

If only one of the ideas I provide can help you improve your teaching or make your studio a better place to work, and thus increase your income, I will feel I have been successful in meeting my goals for writing this book. Ideas and tips can apply to all kinds of doll classes.

Below are some suggestions to help you pull everything together. Many are covered in depth in other parts of the book.

- At the end of a series of classes, hold an open house for family, friends and interested guests.
- At the end of a series of classes, let students judge the dolls they made and award ribbons.
- Have materials available, such as broken or distorted bisque heads, and let students use them to practice painting on the face or setting eyes. Have scraps of felt available for testing eye painting if you're making cloth or felt dolls.
- Teach an entire process—don't start in the middle, even if it's just a demonstration.
- Provide materials so every class member can use the same things, such as equipment, brushes and clean-up tools. This keeps someone from throwing off the speed of the class.
- Uniformity of project and materials makes better classes. The entire class should work at the same speed.
- When giving a demonstration, control questions from the beginning. Ask students to write down a question because it will probably be answered before you finish your lecture or demonstration. This keeps questions from getting you out of sequence.
- Tell and show how to do work, but don't do it for students. *Never* work on a student's piece of work.
- Discuss good and bad points using another doll head you have created. Don't use a student's work.

- Clarify and define terms as you teach. Pass out a vocabulary sheet for each lesson.
- Think and plan your objectives for *each* lesson. When applied to teaching, objective means an aim or anticipated accomplishment.
- Use many *demonstrations*—a demonstration is a method of showing how to do something with actual materials.
- Use some *simulated demonstrations*. A simulated demonstration uses actual materials but has some of the work already done. Use this method when an actual demonstration might give less-than-perfect results.
- Teach students to use materials properly.
- Make worksheets with notes of facts or procedures to be remembered from each lesson. Hand out worksheets so students can make notes on them as they progress.
- Fill your studio or classroom with inspirational material, such as finished dolls.
- At the beginning of each class meeting, quickly outline what you're going to do.
- Outline the entire course on paper so students know the plan.
- Make good models, and use them many times for different classes.
- Make good charts, or have them made, and use them for different classes.
- Have a finished doll of whatever kind you are teaching.
- Tell your students about everything they use and where to buy it.
- Rehearse a demonstration *before* you give it. There's a difference between knowing how to do something and being able to teach it.
- When demonstrating, the angle at which students see is important. Some places I have demonstrated have overhead mirrors or closeup views on closed-circuit television.
- Preview any videocassette doll tapes *before* showing them to students. Make corrections or teach another way if you have found a better method.
- Teach only *one* method that is best for you. Don't mention other methods until your summary.
- At the end of a lesson or demonstration, check where things went wrong and where students had difficulty.
- Do long procedures, or things that could go wrong, ahead of time, then give a simulated demonstration.
- Keep your demonstrations from one year to the next. You'll only have to review them and put together the materials when you're asked to do another. Create handout pages for each demonstration.
- Be sure chairs are arranged so everyone can see and hear you give your demonstration.
- Limit the number of students in a class, and charge more.
- Have an example for everything you wish to show.
- Critique the different stages of students' work. Have students do the critiquing, then give constructive criticism.
- Don't have any tests. Anxiety spoils the fun of doll making.
- Try to make your students enthusiastic about dolls and the doll world. Sell them books so they can read about methods before class and find dolls they will want to make. This will keep your classes filled.
- Be demanding; you must attempt to get each student to do the the very best she can.
- Be well-informed on the latest techniques, sources of material and historical background of dolls.
- Teach all you know.
- Hand out a reading list.
- Speak and teach the language of doll making.
- Know the objectives of each lesson.
- Never show the wrong way to do anything; always show the right way several times.
- Teach the basics, and teach your students well. Start from the beginning, and be sure they understand everything before you go on to something else.
- Help students perfect basics. If the beginning processes are skimped on or left out, everyone will have problems.

Doll Shops

By 1985, doll shops had sprung up all over the country. In the early 1970s, antique dolls were sold with other antiques on side streets. New dolls were sold in toy departments of department stores, and collectable dolls were often discarded. Today, *all* dolls have their places in collections and in fancy shops.

Doll shops are thriving, profitable businesses. Some shops carry only antique dolls. Some carry collectables, and some carry modern and limited-edition dolls. Some shops sell reproduction dolls. Some larger stores carry all types of dolls, along with doll accessories and doll furniture. Stores that once were frequented by a mother and her small child to buy a play doll are now sources for doll collectors.

When building a new business, note trends and changes that have occurred, and anticipate those to come. Before you set up your own shop, study some of the doll shops that are successful. Talk to the owners, and observe their stock and possibly their customers.

In planning *any* kind of doll shop, concentrate and plan well for the following things:

1. *Location.* Always have good parking, and locate in a good, central area that is convenient and safe. Try to find a relatively high traffic area where customers and potential customers pass often.
2. *Store hours.* It's important to keep store hours that are suitable to your customers' needs. Try to remain open during the time your customers can visit you conveniently. You don't want people to have to make special trips to visit you.
3. *Source of supply.* Develop a reliable source of supply from tested or well-established companies. You must be able to purchase items for resale at a suitable discount.

Left: Toys from the period of a doll help create interesting doll displays. This bicycle by Howe sells for about $125. It took metal-working ability and skill to create this bicycle. These were sold at the Oakland Doll Show.

A doll shop needs a good location, variety in stock, appeal to customers and plenty of advertising. Mickie's and Sandy's Antique Dolls in Phoenix fills the requirements. Mickie purchases collections of rare items, usually from Paris, then resells them. Her merchandise includes antique doll corsets, old doll shoes, salesmen's samples and play stoves.

4. *Cost of operation.* You'll have to pay the rent, insurance, utilities, advertising and decorating. Plan for these needs before you think about anything else.
5. *Alterations or decorations.* Plan on how you'll make the place suitable for doll displays.
6. *Shop and studio help.* You may need help in your shop or studio. Look for suitable help in all the areas you need it by advertising in the newspaper or from employment agencies.
7. *Customer potential.* Study and know who your customers are.

SUPPLIER-OPERATED DOLL SHOPS

Some of the most successful doll shops are operated by a supplier. One example is the shop owned by Joyce Wolf. She makes reproduction dolls, original dolls, her own molds and all kinds of accessories to sell.

Making your own supply of salable doll items isn't easy. It takes management, family cooperation and hired help. This type of shop probably shows the greatest profits of any doll shop, except for antique-doll shops.

Supplier-operated shops often have family help, with several family members producing items or working in the shop. Some family members serve in several capacities by working in the shop and producing the product.

Most doll artists must concentrate on making dolls, but they are creative people and can think of many things they could sell with dolls as items or services. This type of doll shop often starts as an extra room at home or a room or two on a side street. If the shop is good, people will find it. Sometimes these shops expand so quickly and business is so good they move almost immediately to a good, mainstream location. But many doll shops have found this is unnecessary and have chosen to keep a known location.

RUNNING AN ANTIQUE-DOLL SHOP

You can't be in business or run an antique-doll shop without the basic ingredient—dolls. Dolls must be purchased at a price that can be increased enough for resale to make a profit for you. Some basic rules to follow when buying dolls for resale include:
1. Don't buy dolls from local dealers. Their prices aren't low enough for resale, and local traffic will already have bought the best dolls.
2. Don't feel you have to travel all over the country. There are good dolls in *all* areas of the country.
3. Don't buy more than 10% of your opening stock from one auction or seller. This protects against too-high a price paid on the wrong dolls.
4. Buy quality dolls. Many low-priced or poor dolls can discourage better customers from the beginning.
5. Take time to search and stockpile dolls for months before opening.

To get started, run a small advertisement in your local newspaper. State you are interested in buying dolls made before 1930.

Your purchases will be made from many different people. As a beginner, offer what you believe is about 1/3 of the price you can sell the doll for when it is cleaned and put in your shop. This gives you some leeway for mistakes and unnoticed flaws. Fine-quality dolls, in good selling condition, may be purchased for as much as 60% of your final selling price. If you're sure of what you're buying, you can pay a higher price.

Many doll collectors use accessories in their doll cases. Dealers can mark these items up for a nice profit, so you might want to consider carrying doll accessories if you own a doll shop.

Just because a doll is old does not make it worth more or make it more desirable. You must study old dolls, the doll world, buying and selling before you can be aware of what is selling for what price.

Try to select popular dolls for rapid turnover. Some dolls, with minor faults, can be sold at lower-than-normal prices; they are good for new or less-particular collectors. But keep in mind that an unusual doll, a rare doll or a perfect doll will outsell a commonplace dolly-faced doll anytime.

Join a local doll club. Visit shops or dealers who sell dolls in your area or within a 100-mile radius. Attend doll shows or doll functions within a day's drive. Attend doll auctions that are within easy travel distances. Plan to attend major auctions held in different parts of the country so you will be aware of which dolls are selling and their market value.

Auction buying for your shop can turn into one of your biggest sources of supply. Auction houses sell many of the country's large doll collections and even sell out closed doll museums. Plan ahead on what may be good buys for resale.

Plan how you'll get any dolls you buy home. Determine how you will pay for them. Auctions on the East Coast often last 2 days. Midwest auctions can last 1 day, but West-Coast auctions are more apt to be a 4-hour evening event.

A traveling auction, such as Theriault's, usually has the same setup for each auction, and they are held in and around big cities all over the country. Review the rules for attending an auction in another book I wrote for HPBooks, *Doll Collecting for Fun and Profit*.

Many antique-doll dealers depend on auctions for their general supply of dolls. Some of their buying is even done by absentee bidding. *Absentee bidding* is a bid for a particular doll submitted by mail before the auction. Not all doll auctions allow absentee bids. I feel it's a little dangerous to purchase a doll by absentee bid from only a photograph and description if there is no chance of returning it.

Learn how to do minor doll repairs, such as stringing, cleaning, wig work and eye setting. You'll save money and help yourself if you can do many minor repairs. My book *Doll Costuming*, also published by HPBooks, contains information on doll repairs and costuming.

Don't buy dolls that need extensive repair—these repairs must be done by an expert. Your money will be tied up while the doll is being repaired. If you can't costume a doll yourself, have someone lined up who will do this for you. If costuming is something you can do well and you enjoy it, it will be to your advantage.

Most antique-doll shops sell retail only. Some shops advertise that their prices are wholesale, but they are unable to give the 30 to 40% discount of true wholesale. These shops often give a 10 or 15% discount off the price of

ERNEST AND BAILEY

"Couturier-costumer" Bailey and "Modiste to the Dolls" Ernest share the same booth at many doll shows to show their racks of doll fashions. Each costume is carefully made of the finest materials, and these couturiers have found sales exceptionally good. Both ladies rely on their skills as seamstresses and designers to produce costumes that please the most discriminating doll collectors.

the doll to the trade (customers with a resale number, whether they actively sell dolls or not).

A number of years ago, container-buying of dolls from Europe was possible. (These were not the 40-foot containers used for general antiques.) I purchased a couple of containers of dolls from Denmark. This practice has nearly come to a halt, but you may still find some advertisements for container lots in some dealer-oriented antique periodicals, such as *Antique Dealer, Antique Trader Weekly* or *Collector News*.

Some doll dealers still go to Europe and bring home enough dolls to pay for the trip and their travel expenses. There are good doll auctions in Europe, but prices are not necessarily better than in the United States.

DOLL SERVICES

Many services can go hand-in-hand with an antique-doll shop; these may help increase the number of people coming into your shop and help build your reputation. Probably one of the best services you can provide is the general repair of dolls.

Another service offered by antique-doll shops is selling dolls by telephone or by mail. Dealers call their favorite customers when they get a great doll. They also sell dolls to customers through the mail.

Some doll dealers offer a buying service. They attend auctions and purchase dolls on order for a customer. Here the dealer may take only a 20% markup because she will have no outlay of money, and she takes no risk. A dealer may also search for a particular doll for a customer from other dealers, at conventions, shows or even on the telephone. In this case, the shop owner will take her expenses, plus a 20% markup.

When the owner of an antique-doll shop purchases a large doll collection, she can assign part of it to a doll auction. She will get some immediate returns—perhaps all her cash outlay back.

Many dealers purchase an entire doll collection—this is where the dealer gets the best price on dolls. It's wise to advertise you will purchase collections, large or small. You may wonder how a dealer comes up with a price on 50 dolls or 100 dolls. Everyone has their own method, but one method is discussed below.

If the collection is small, the dealer examines the dolls, finds the best one, figures what she can sell that one for and offers that price for the entire collection. She may use the same method on a large collection, using the total for the three or four best dolls.

Advertise in newspapers, doll magazines and through the mail saying you will purchase complete collections, and offer to purchase, pack and pick up dolls from estates—with immediate payment. Immediate payment is what attracts a person who wants to sell the dolls because when dolls are sent to auction, it may take 6 months before payment is received.

ACCESSORIES

Most antique-doll shops carry old doll furniture, carriages and other accessories for the attractive arrangement of dolls. Accessories can often make a double sale. Much depends on your ability as shop owner to set up dolls so a doll and furniture look as though they were made for each other.

Keep copies of all the latest price guides for dolls and doll items. Even better than price guides are illustrated auction catalogs with the price an item actually sold for. Auction prices are *actual* selling prices; price guides are *estimates* of selling prices.

Books—As an antique-doll dealer, you'll need

many reference books. These are not of value unless you know what's in them. Antique dolls are still being discovered and being brought into shops for identification.

It's wise for a reproduction-doll shop to have the same books. It helps to show a customer what the antique doll, from which the reproduction doll was made, is selling for. Reproduction-doll sellers need to know about antique dolls. Doll books are important to *any* doll entrepreneur. When I started in the doll world, there were few books available. Today, hundreds of books are available on all types of dolls.

Selling doll books is a great addition to any kind of doll shop. Doll books are a natural addition to your sales line and generate additional income. When an antique-doll dealer purchases an entire doll collection, often there is a library of doll books in the same place. These used books—some out-of-print—make a great addition to the stock of the shop. New books should also be stocked; selling books helps make additional sales.

Old books and magazines, such as *Peterson's Magazine* and *Godey's Lady Book*, are still being sold in antique shops. These types of publications are a wonderful source of costumes for dolls and should be carried by every antique-doll shop. Hand-colored prints found in old magazines and books are a source of costume design and an added decoration to a doll room or doll cabinet. Prints might be reproduced for sale, which could be a decorative item for a doll collector.

Another item that goes well with antique dolls and reproduction dolls is doll plates. People can have the rarest or most expensive dolls on plates. Some customers like to match a doll and plate. Plates are another way to collect dolls. They are a profitable item to sell, along with the dolls, because about 40 to 50% of each plate sale is profit. Dolls shown on plates are antique dolls, so they do not clash with other antiques.

You must think like a collector. Where will you put the purchased doll? Did you sell a chair

Doll auction houses, such as Sotheby's, Theriaults, Cohen and Withington, put out catalogs before an auction. Catalogs can sell from $12 to $22.

or case for the doll? Can a framed print or plate be hung with the doll? Do you have a book with the history of these dolls? Multiply your sales by thinking of everything you can sell along with the doll *before* you sell a doll!

LOCATION OF THE SHOP

Doll shops need to be located in an area where customers feel safe and where they won't hesitate to go alone. One famous restaurant owner says his success is due to one thing—his restaurant is located in an affluent area.

This might also make a success of your doll shop. Taking a lesson from car dealers who locate within blocks of each other, a doll shop should be located with other doll shops, antique shops or doll studios. People love to visit several shops while they are in the area. The advertising your neighbor does may bring in

Doll shops must be placed in good locations. The Doll Nook is convenient and inviting and holds classes in the back. Even small shops can do a great business.

customers for you. Sometimes advertising can be done together. Special events held by one shop or a group of shops can bring in new customers.

ADVERTISING ANTIQUE DOLLS

Some progressive antique-doll shops advertise in national doll magazines; dolls they wish to sell are pictured in black and white. With the doll is a description and price. Most of these shops offer a few-day-return-privilege and credit-card buying. Most dolls are ordered by telephone.

In these advertisements, doll collectors are made aware of old dolls they can buy and their prices, and they learn of a shop they can visit when traveling in that area.

If you're going to advertise in a magazine, be sure the points in the list in the next column are included in the description, along with a good photo. Study other ads, and you'll soon know what is good and what will sell dolls.

When you write your ad, make the description as clear and concise as possible. Include the following information:

- Height of doll
- Markings
- Type and color of eyes
- Open or closed mouth
- Applied or pierced ears
- Type of wig
- Condition and color of costume
- Anything special, such as character face
- Price

Some shops that advertise in national magazines also have a mailing list. They send their customers a one- or two-page, black-and-white flyer with photographs of dolls for sale. You can create and mail your own flyers on a regular basis or when you have new groups of dolls to sell.

Some doll shops sell one or two dolls or a whole collection for a commission, usually about 10%. Some of these doll shops, like Julia Melton's, can turn a doll collection into dollars very quickly. Julia does it by telephone, magazine ads and using a mailing list. She also has a shop.

A friend of ours, Fay Davis of Tubac, Arizona, is a doll dealer who has done some different kinds of promotions. For many years, she held a tea party for the doll people in her area. She sent out attractive invitations to more people than her home could hold. The time of the tea party on the invitation was scheduled from 1 to 4 p.m. in the afternoon, so people arrived all through the afternoon. She prepared tea and fancy foods. Everyone knew she had just gotten in a collection of dolls to sell. She always set up a bargain table of $10 doll items—her "junk" she says.

This was a novel way of selling dolls, and it worked. Fay had little overhead. She didn't take a table at a doll show or go with her dolls to an expensive convention. She paid little for advertising costs, yet expensive dolls were sold, commanding the same price they would anywhere.

At a large doll show or doll convention, you can buy any kind of doll you want—from a baby doll to a lady doll, from plastic to bisque, from 1850 to modern.

ROBERT RAIKES

There are only a few doll makers making their living from carving dolls from wood. One very successful wood carver is Robert Raikes. He makes carousel horses and wood dolls. He designed a teddy bear with a wood face that has been sold to a toy company. Raikes' success is due to his carving and designing abilities. It is also due to his ability to see change and produce a product that has a chance to be successful in the market.

SELLING AT DOLL SHOWS AND DOLL CONVENTIONS

Doll magazines are filled with advertisements for forthcoming doll shows. Some doll shows are huge and held in major convention centers; some are small, local events.

Only a few dolls are now sold at antique shows. On the East Coast, the large 3-day flea markets and covered weekend flea markets are a source to buy dolls or a place to sell them. The owner of an antique-doll shop may feel these flea markets are opportunities to build her reputation and make numerous sales. At a flea market, more people will pass a booth in a day than will visit a shop in a month.

At regional conventions, I have seen booths of good-quality dolls completely sold out. At some local shows, I have talked to antique-doll dealers who have not sold a single doll. Some areas are better than others for selling old dolls—much depends on the activities of local doll clubs. Doll people have a tendency to buy many times from the same dealer. I buy from dealers across the country whom I have never met, as well as many I have known for years. I have confidence in these dealers and trust them to sell me good dolls. Many doll collectors use this same mail-order telephone method to acquire the best dolls.

Traveling to shows can mean added expense. You may want to keep the shop open while you're gone. You'll have travel expenses and booth-rental fees. You may feel you'll need to add a bit to the price of your dolls to cover this, or you may feel the extra sales will more than cover the expenses.

There are "antique-doll shops" without a store. These are the dealers who join a circuit, and shows are scheduled one after the other as they travel from city to city around the country. These circuits are more prevalent in the winter, when they travel to the warm vacation places in the South and Southwest.

Sometimes this type of travel allows you to pick up dolls in different parts of the country. You may be able to advertise in local newspapers that you are interested in buying dolls in advance of the show's arrival.

To maximize the benefits to you, follow the guidelines listed below when showing at a circuit show:

1. The date must not conflict with other large, crowd-drawing functions in the area.
2. The sponsor must know how to advertise to draw a good crowd.
3. As a doll dealer, you must have something outstanding or different, such as a mechanical doll, to attract the crowd's attention to your booth.

LIEBLING
(My Darling)
K★R 117-a
by Peck-Gandre
First in our series
of collectible paper dolls
Enclosed
Mein Liebling
a hand painted
18 inch German
ball-joint doll.
Authentic clothing
designs include:
6 hand painted outfits
and
6 black and white
outfits to
be colored.

4. Talk to potential customers—don't read a book or visit with other dealers.
5. Don't allow too many people to fill your booth at any one time.
6. Bring 3 times as much as you plan to sell. You can't sell what you don't have.
7. Figure a way to get people to register in your booth to let you know what they're looking for. This will help in the future, and you may build up telephone or mail-order trade this way.
8. Keep extremely valuable dolls covered with domes or in cases. Tiny items should also be kept in glass cases.
9. Make your booth as attractive as possible.

A lot of doll business is done between dealers. It's always wise to set up early, then make the rounds of the other booths before the show opens. Buying and selling among dealers is planned and some trading goes on, but this is unwise because someone always looses.

COLLECTING FOR SALES

Some doll collectors collect series of dolls or dolls that have something in common, then resell the collection to make a profit. This is done more in composition and plastic dolls than in bisque dolls.

Some dealers buy any kind of doll, in any condition, as long as it is inexpensive. They clean the dolls, repair them, costume them and resell them at a good profit.

Some people look for super collectors' dolls—these dolls appreciate about 20% a year. They hold the dolls until they find a collector who is looking for that particular, special doll and will pay almost anything to get it.

As you can see, there's more to owning and running an antique-doll shop than just buying a few dolls and opening your doors. To be successful, you must plan, plan, plan—then plan some more!

Left: Paper dolls are popular. We find pages of well-designed paper dolls in magazines by many creative designers, such as Pat Stall and Peggy Jo Rosamond. This cardboard doll, and others of similar size, is made by Linda Peck and Marilyn Gandré. Read their "Dollionaire" story on page 45.

Reproduction-Doll Shops

A shop that sells reproduction dolls (exact copies of antique dolls) is usually one of two types. It is the *shop of a doll artist* that exists in connection with her doll-making studio, or it is a *shop that sells reproduction dolls* by many artists. Both types of shops can and do make substantial profits, but there's more profit in selling your own dolls if you're the doll artist.

It's difficult for one person to produce enough dolls in a great enough variety to supply all demands. This is especially true if the dolls are exceptionally good. Sometimes a doll maker will sell dolls made by several of her best students to meet demands of her customers.

To sell enough dolls to support a shop, reproduction dolls must be:

- Well-made.
- Appropriately dressed.
- Beautifully wigged.
- True reproduction (an *exact copy* of an antique doll).
- From many different molds—German and French dolls represented.
- Baby dolls, child dolls or lady dolls—a variety for different collectors.
- Different prices, from economical to expensive.

A reproduction-doll shop should, and usually does, carry doll accessories, such as wigs, costumes, bonnets and any other items that sell with dolls. Think of your customer and what she will want. Often a grandmother will want to purchase dolls for her grandchildren, then pick out wigs and dresses to suit her fancy. Some people want to pick out a doll that looked like they did as a child, then wig it and dress it as they were dressed. *Imagination* on your part—as the shop operator—is a vital part of your success.

Left: 30-inch antique R.D. doll helped pay for itself when a mold was made of her head. The doll's value is a little over $5,000.

Jamie Englert's reproduction doll.

There are two main reasons for the success of reproduction-doll shops. The products for making reproduction dolls are much finer than those from which antique dolls were made—a reproduction doll made today can be finer than an antique doll. The fine porcelain, refined china paints and reproduction bodies available today are more substantial and perfect. Along with the increased knowledge of doll making, these facts make reproduction dolls (or replicas) something to be desired.

In addition, prices of antique dolls have soared until even the poorest, tiniest antique doll can cost over $100. Doll collectors find many antique dolls are out of their price range. The faces of antique Bru, Jumeau and A.T. dolls appeal to collectors—one solution for these collectors is to buy the beloved dolls as reproductions or replicas. There are few expensive antique dolls still available—but there are many collectors. The rarity of antique dolls adds to the desirability of good reproduction dolls and shops that sell them.

The main ingredient for a reproduction-doll shop to be financially successful is the quality of the dolls that are sold. As I mentioned earlier, you must have an assortment of types and prices of dolls, but *all* dolls must be of the best craftsmanship. Dolls must have bisque work and painting that is as good or better than the antique doll's. You must be true to the original doll—don't substitute Oriental bodies or bisque bodies where a composition body was originally used.

When costuming the dolls, look at old dolls. Put French costumes on French dolls. Use simple, childlike costumes on the K(star)Rs. Use my *Doll Costuming* book, published by HPBooks, for reference. Be sure to dress dolls correctly.

As the operator of a reproduction-doll shop, you must also have an extensive knowledge of antique dolls. You should know the story and background of every original old doll that has been an inspiration for every reproduction doll.

Your customer will lose something if she buys a reproduction Bye-Lo baby doll without knowing something about Grace Storey Putnam. Some faces of the K(star)Rs cannot truly be appreciated unless you know about the move to use real children for doll models.

Owners need to know which original dolls were copied, so reproduction French dolls need the names of the dolls from which they were copied, such as Bru, Jumeau or Steiner. Sales will increase as new collectors become aware of the different types of dolls produced by the doll masters. It is through education that your customers—the collectors—will want to expand their collections.

Books—A big asset to any reproduction-doll shop is the sale of doll books. These books have been found to work in several ways to increase overall sales in reproduction-doll shops.

1. Books increase a collector's knowledge of antique dolls. A collector's background knowledge of dolls will be expanded, and she will want more dolls to represent many great doll masters.

2. In books, collectors will find, and maybe fall in love with, dolls they feel they *must* add to their collection.
3. Collectors may find dolls that looked like one they had as a child or one that looked like them as a child. Their search begins, and your shop could be the first place they will hunt for more dolls.
4. In doll books about making reproduction dolls, collectors will find photos of dolls whose molds are available or dolls you have available in your shop.
5. Collectors love to see photographs of their dolls in books—they may buy the book *and* the doll.
6. Some collectors will read and understand how specialized and complicated it is to make a doll. They may develop a deep appreciation for the doll artist and her work. Only 1 in 300 will decide she can make a doll.

Another facet that helps in the success of a reproduction-doll shop is to be able to fill the special needs of any customer coming through your door. Collectors may want dolls you don't have on display. They will want special items for their dolls. As shop owner, be prepared to fill these requests. Be prepared to go above and beyond your present stock to satisfy your customers. They'll appreciate it and return to you for help in the future.

REPRODUCTION-DOLL SHOPS

There are some important things to consider when you set up a shop. In addition to how nice a shop looks, you must consider the physical set up of the store. The shop must be clean, attractive and inviting. Dolls must be well-displayed, with information about a doll readily available. An eye-catching display window may stop passersby. The shop must be well-lighted. Have comfortable chairs available for older customers or tired shoppers. Keep a good supply of books, magazines and other doll literature so people can browse through them. Make sure prices are well-marked. Make up a slogan and logo for your shop.

Marque reproduction for sale at the Oakland, California show.

DOLLS FOR A DOLL SHOP

Many doll shops purchase dolls made in Japan and Korea; these dolls are made for large companies in the United States. I have asked people in shops why they carry these particular dolls when beautiful, true-reproduction dolls are available for purchase here in this country.

I've gotten two answers. First, foreign dolls are less expensive. The second answer is more complicated—and one a doll maker needs to know about, think about and act upon.

Shop owners say American doll makers and doll artists are difficult to work with. Owners say doll makers won't guarantee to produce a certain number of reproduction dolls by a certain time. They produce a few dolls, then never fill the following orders. Or doll makers reduce the quality of their dolls after the first few dolls, such as using poorer eyes or wigs. Other complaints were that special holiday orders didn't come in as promised, and individual orders for a customer took as long as 3 months.

Understanding between the shop owner and doll maker is essential. The doll maker is the one who must adjust and be flexible if she wants to have a continuing, profitable business. As a doll maker, you must adjust your time and production to fit the shop owner's customers.

Doll makers have many problems securing the best wigs, eyes, shoes and clothing. They have production problems of flecks in porcelain, warpage and getting proper bodies. But you must solve these problems; they must not become the problems or concerns of the shop owner.

Carefully think about the prices you charge for you reproduction dolls; prices should be fair and competitive so shop owner and doll maker can make a profit. Non-standard pricing and changing of prices makes it difficult for a shop owner to work with a doll maker.

Imported dolls are not the same as our lovely reproduction dolls, and I feel it's a shame to see people buying imports when they could have something much better. And our doll makers need to sell their dolls! If you want to sell your dolls to a doll shop on a regular basis, answer the following questions honestly.

1. Do you know how many dolls you can produce and complete in a month?
2. Do you know exactly how much these dolls cost to produce and costume?
3. Do you know how many hours it takes to make a particular number of dolls?
4. Do you have an hourly wage?
5. Do you have sources of supply that are reliable?
6. Do you do exactly as you promise in the way of special dolls?
7. Do you procrastinate and take 3 months to get out a special doll?
8. Do you listen to the shop owner when she tells you what her customers want?
9. Is your mind always on what will sell, or do you do your own thing?
10. Will you tire after making several replicas of the same doll?
11. Can you get good help if your orders become too large for you to handle alone?
12. Do you have enough money to complete your first order (and wait for the payment from shop owner—maybe 30 days)?

Get these problems and questions straightened out in your own mind before you decide how much you can do for whom by when. Sell your dolls to a shop with confidence, and do it in an orderly fashion. Make money!

PRODUCTION

Many of the problems I've just described are tied to production methods. Doll makers often begin making one doll at a time and continue this slow procedure. To produce dolls for a doll shop, you must put some "factory methods" to work for you.

Many things will help cut down on the total time it takes to make a doll. Below is a list of shortcuts I have discovered:

- Pour 2 week's or 1 month's supply of doll heads at one time.
- Clean and prepare eyeholes all at once.
- Use large trays, and line up your work.
- Select patterns and order bodies, wigs, eyes and shoes for the entire job when you start pouring heads.
- Begin work on, or have someone else do it, costumes from the very beginning so the clothing is finished when the dolls are finished.

Old-Time Ginny Dolls

The ever popular 8in (20.3cm) *Ginny* makes another debut, this time for Meritus Industries, Inc. Looking more like the original *Ginny* by Vogue Dolls, this new all-vinyl doll comes in 12 different styles. An exciting new addition to *The World of Ginny*™ is the Chinese Porcelain Collection featuring three different styles of *Ginny* all done in Chinese porcelain.

Four limited edition *Ginnys* of fine porcelain are presented in *The Heritage Collection: Southern Belle, Party Time, Christmas Spirit* and *Holiday Deluxe*.

Above: To get an article about, or mention of, an event in the newspaper is great advertising. Many doll people owe some of their success to news articles.

Right: When you create an ad, don't skimp in the size or quality. Use good photos, like this one, to show detail and color.

You can see what I'm getting at—complete each operation on the entire group of dolls before you go on to something else. It will take much less time, and it will make the dolls better. For example, you've mixed up brown china paint for eyebrows. It's working well, and your strokes are steady today—so paint *all* the eyebrows. This saves paint-mixing time, brush-cleaning time and all the time it takes to get things assembled for the job.

Use this do-it-all procedure for everything, even sewing up the sleeves of dresses. Even a small production of six dolls can be speeded up and will cost you less in time, effort and materials if you employ some factory methods.

Part of the speed-up in production is due to the setup and organization of your doll studio. Some doll shops are a mess, and I wonder how anything comes out as nicely as it does. Organize your shop so work flows from department to department. If the shop is tiny and you have to pour molds, pour many molds, then clean up. Use the space you have efficiently and effectively.

Another way to increase production of a single doll is to have several molds available. This isn't easy if you have to purchase the molds. If you aren't pouring the same molds, use molds of heads that are about the same size. You may find certain dolls are easier to produce together, even if they're different. You can put more heads in the kiln if they're about the same size. You can also save time painting if you use the same colors.

ADVERTISING SUGGESTIONS

Advertising is necessary for a doll shop to succeed. Most doll shops must advertise locally for walk-in customers. Many shops also advertise nationally in doll magazines to make greater profits through mail-order business.

The results of advertising are as intriguing to the onlooker as to the advertiser. Advertising has become a way of life. If you're an amateur, you probably don't know how or what to advertise, but by studying other ads, you'll soon learn.

Most advertising is not a single advertisement but a series of ads or an ad campaign. Poor advertising may result in poor results; super advertising may be the best thing to happen to your company or shop.

Try some of the following ideas to help with your advertising if you are new in the business. Always read competitors' ads, other literature and whatever is available. You'll stay aware of what is happening—you can always learn something.

- There are some excellent books and pamphlets on advertising available at bookstores and libraries.
- Doll-magazine advertising departments will help you with your advertisements. Have all your information together *before* you approach them for assistance about advertising in their magazine.
- Press releases *you* write are a good way to introduce something new, such as a special doll made just for your company. "What's-new" columns in doll magazines may also mention your company or product.
- Answer all inquires from your ads, and sign letters yourself—add the personal touch. Telephone where it is considered advisable, such as to answer questions that might sell a doll or make a return customer.
- Make reprints of your advertisements or any writeups about you, and add them to your mailings. Use reprints as direct mail for your customers.
- Your ad must attract enough attention so potential customers will read about your services or product. Good illustrations and eye-catching print for headlines are important.
- Don't be afraid you will overuse the words *new, now, save* or *announcing*. They attract a reader's attention.
- Be honest—don't exaggerate. Tell a customer how he or she can benefit from your product.
- Always assume you'll get an order with a follow-up phone call. Don't hesitate to ask for an order.
- Many advertisers repeat ads; this does something for their image. People associate the ad with the company; an advertisement can continue to pick up customers.
- Look at your advertising as though you were the customer—would you buy your product?
- Explain your objectives, and keep your help informed about advertising. It will help them sell your products if they know what you're planning.
- Coordinate your marketing program so advertising, promotion of sales and public relations all work together.
- Don't decrease advertising at the first sign of a decline in business. Outshine the competition by consistent advertising.
- Look for new and exciting ways to advertise. Don't hesitate to be creative and different.
- Advertising should be persuasive and logical, like any good sales presentation.
- Be sure your material is ready early for magazine or newspaper advertising. Schedule the ad, put it on your calendar and get everything ready in plenty of time. Material will be better if you have time to work on it and are not rushed.
- Use a logo, certain styles in printing or certain forms of ads—customers will recognize your ad in an instant.
- Don't skimp in the size or quality of your advertisements. Advertising is the backbone of the doll business.
- Put forth your best effort in developing your ad campaign.

BILL O'CONNOR

It's good business practice to apply what you already know. Bill O'Connor used to be a window designer, making mannequins. Now he's retired, and he uses the same techniques and same materials to make his dolls. Even fabrics show his artistic ability—when he can't find an edging, print or lace to suit him, he paints or makes what he needs.

PROMOTING THE REPRODUCTION-DOLL SHOP

The most important aspects of success for a new shop is advertising. Set aside a certain percentage of your budget for advertising, such as 10%. This may seem like a lot, but it is important. Divide your advertising budget up into many different areas, including newspaper, radio, television, handbills, local bulletin boards and maybe local club bulletins.

Develop Themes—I am often asked how to write a good ad. First, I develop a theme. I choose something that is appealing, such as grandparents, creativity, fun, artistry, value, gifts. Other themes might include "What happened to your early childhood dolls?" "Look in the attic trunk—you might find a treasure." Play up the value of antique dolls.

Hold an Open House—Advertise to get people to bring in their old dolls for appraisal or some other reasons, such as a contest. This is one good way to get people reinterested in dolls. This can be done with an *open house*. People who have an interest meet other people, and often the interest multiplies. You might even be able to get a doll club started.

Write to all the doll-supply houses. They may supply prizes and literature for your open house. They may also help you advertise.

Hold a contest. Give a prize for the oldest doll, prettiest doll, ugliest doll, handmade doll and various other categories. Have a contest for someone to write in 500 words or less "My Favorite Doll," "My Favorite Doll Story," "What Happened to My Childhood Doll." Give a substantial prize, such as $50 or $100, for the best story. Use the story in your advertising; you'll be surprised how much interest it will create.

Or sponsor an essay contest for children writing about dolls. Children probably won't be your customers, but their parents may be. This helps create interest and enthusiasm for doll collecting.

Try working with your local newspaper to create a contest, such as 25 questions on antique dolls. Start with easy questions, and progress to very difficult ones. These questions will start everyone thinking about dolls. Make the prize worthwhile—you'll be surprised at the interest it can generate.

Use Local Publicity—Perhaps a local radio or television show or a newspaper will report about you. This is some of the best advertising you can get.

Doll Programs—Check with local women's clubs, and arrange to hold a doll program for them. Clubs are always looking for free programs. Bank clubs, church groups and senior-citizen groups are also excellent places to begin.

Displays—Offer to do a window display at a bank or Chamber of Commerce. You can display some of your reproduction dolls to create interest among the public.

Dolls Shows—Work with local, non-profit organizations, and help them raise money by putting on a doll show.

TRUBIT INC.

Solid carbide bits to drill porcelain in 1/8-, 3/32- and 1/16-inch holes (for use in a moto tool) are new. These bits will drill holes for earrings in fired porcelain or any other holes you forgot to make in the greenware. Here Trubit *found a need*, then filled it—this is always a sound business practice.

SELLING DOLLS AND DOLL ITEMS

No time is better than *right now* to try to sell your homemade dolls and doll items. The market for American-made reproduction and original dolls is flourishing, especially because prices of antique dolls are so high. Nearly every state has doll shows, and more focus is being placed on reproduction dolls.

This widespread interest in "American" dolls doesn't mean you will automatically make money. Whatever your product—from tiny all-bisque dolls to French fashion dolls—it must appeal to the buying public. Your products must compete in price and still bring you a fair return for your costs and your time.

You may need help setting up a doll business. On the following pages are some things for you to consider.

Reproduction dolls lend themselves to creativeness in costuming. These dolls are called *Robin's Dolls.*

1. Decide whether your dolls and doll items are salable.

The first step in making the transition from hobbyist to professional is to begin thinking about your products as salable items in a *very* competitive market. The more you know about your market, the better your chances are for success.

Begin with research to see where and how your dolls or doll items will fit in the market and what your competition is offering. Visit doll shows that sell doll products similar to yours. Observe what is selling—costumes, sizes of dolls, quality and price. Survey doll publications, and study advertisements. Talk to and write members of other doll clubs.

Next, join organizations, such as the Doll Artisan Guild (DAG), an international organization for porcelain-doll artists, or the United Federation of Doll Clubs (UFDC) (the largest doll-collector club in the United States). Each group publishes a magazine to keep you informed about what is happening, what is selling and what is being collected.

2. Determine whether you should sell your doll items wholesale or retail.

Retail is selling directly to customers, such as in your shop or at doll shows. *Wholesale* is selling your dolls and doll items to others, who will resell them to customers.

You must decide what size and type of business would work best for you. Make your business fit your spare time and money situation. If you decide to sell your product retail, you'll have to collect and pay state tax on each sale. Sometimes city tax must also be paid.

You need to find out what is required in your state. Register your business so you are a legitimate small business; that way you can buy supplies tax-free at wholesale prices. In most states, you are given a state tax license or resale number. This number is used when you purchase something you will resell in your business.

Bookkeeping is also very important. Each day you must record expenses and income, no matter how small, for income-tax purposes. If you make a profit in 2 out of 5 consecutive years, you're in business; otherwise, it's a hobby for pleasure, not profit. Once you begin to sell, you must declare your income and pay tax on any profits. With a hobby, you're allowed to offset income with expenses only up to the amount of that income. In a business, you can't claim expenses that exceed your income. It's always good to check out everything with an accountant *before* you begin.

3. Decide whether you will go into business with a partner or by yourself.

You have three choices—run the business yourself, enter into a partnership or set up a corporation. See page 44 for more information on each situation. The first two situations are easiest to set up, but you have no protection against legal action. Each partner is responsible for everything that happens in the business, so be careful. A lawyer must set up a corporation of three or more people; a corporation protects you personally.

4. *Plan how you will price your products.*

Pricing dolls and doll items is the next step. Setting the right price in the beginning is not easy. You must work out how you do things to make prices comparable to your competitors'. To determine how much you should charge, try the following:

- On paper, list the cost of everything you need to create the finished product.
- Figure out how much it would cost to hire someone to make your products by the hour.
- Determine how much your work area and utilities cost—rent, electricity, packaging, typing and any other costs you would accrue.
- Take the cost of these things for 10 dolls or doll items, and divide it by 10. Add this figure to whatever you feel you should have for a profit, and you will have a basic selling price.

If you sell retail, you can usually double your costs to get your selling price. If you are selling wholesale, then you must make your money by selling more products at a lower cost. Shops usually double the price of the wholesaler. If you sell retail, be sure to advertise because your sales depend on it.

Making stamp blocks with doll motifs is an entire business for one California company.

SOME DOLL ITEMS TO MAKE FOR SALE

Below and on the following page is a list of some items you might want to consider making that go along with dolls. Be creative—I'm sure you can think of many more!

Advertising dolls
Baby baskets
Baby-doll bonnets
Bears for dolls
Birthday cakes of dolls
Bodies—leather, cloth, felt
Bookmarks
Bouquets of flowers for dolls
Cards—birthday, Christmas, get-well
Children's quilts with dolls on them
Christmas-tree ornaments with dolls
Clothes racks for doll clothes
Copies of folk-art dolls
Doll aprons (men's and ladies')
Doll bank to save for a new doll
Doll books for collectors
Doll books for doll makers
Doll calendars
Doll chairs in antique styles
Doll costumes
Doll dinnerware
Doll houses
Doll patchwork quilts
Doll prints
Doll quilts
Doll smocks
Doll stands
Doll stockings and socks
Doll-dish molds
Doll-dress hangers
Doll-house accessories
Doll-house fixtures & lighting
Doll-house furniture
Doll-inventory books
Fancy ribbons for doll costumes, hats and hair
Fans, muffs and fur pieces for lady dolls
Felt dolls
Figurines
Fobs for key rings
Folk costumes for dolls

Framed pictures of dolls
French bonnets of cloth or straw
Gift boxes
Glass globes for displaying dolls
Hat boxes
Hat flowers in small sizes
Holiday dolls
Items decorated with doll photos
Jewelry with dolls on it
Lady-doll stands
Limited-edition doll plates
Marionettes
Memo pads with pictures of dolls
Miniature French hats for doll-house dolls
Music box with dolls on cover
Music box with dressed porcelain doll on lid
Needlepoint or needlework design
Old prints found in books, reprinted
Original doll-house dolls
Paper dolls from old dolls
Paper dolls from original dolls
Party placemats, cup, napkins
Patterns for cloth dolls
Patterns for costumes
Pewter castings of dolls
Pillows
Pins with dolls on them
Plates with dolls for adults
Playing cards

Posters
Pull toys for dolls
Puzzles from doll photos
Repair and restorative materials
Replica doll-house dolls
Reprints of old catalogs and magazines
Reprints of old cloth dolls
Reproduction bodies
Reproduction doll carriages
Reproduction dolls
Scarves with doll designs for adults
Shoes for dolls
Special doll charms, necklaces, bracelets
Stickers with pictures of dolls on them
3-dimensional doll items in a frame
T-shirts with dolls on them
Tools for making dolls
Tools for repairing dolls
Tote bags with pictures of dolls on them
Toy animals from antique designs
Trims and laces for doll costumes
Trunks for doll clothes
Umbrellas
Wax dolls
Wigs
Wood dolls
Wrapping paper printed with doll drawings
Writing paper
Yard goods for French dolls

MARTHA WATKINS

Martha Watkins is a studio owner and distributor for Seeley Ceramics, but this doesn't keep her from adding her own ideas to her business. Martha may run the only studio that holds seminars on china dolls. She also caters to the doll costumer; she carries 20 to 30 bolts of different types of silk, braids, trims, silk ribbon, cotton lace and batiste. These materials are difficult to find, and they bring in trade from doll makers and doll collectors from far away.

Right: Platform rocker is a copy of an old piece of furniture by a furniture company. It is incised *Dodgson, Furn-Mfg* with a sun and a *D* inside. Doll collectors and doll makers use furniture to display their dolls. This could be a sideline for a company that has the knowledge and equipment to make these products. Doll is Steiner.

Doll Services

Many people make money from dolls—and they don't collect, buy, sell or make dolls. These people are involved in *doll services*. Many doll studios and antique- and reproduction-doll shops add services to their shops. Many services are full-time jobs, and those involved in them make a good living.

PROMOTIONS—SHOWS AND CONVENTIONS

Today, there are people who work full time promoting doll shows and doll conventions. Many doll shows are so well-attended by buyers *and* sellers that three or four good shows a year can earn someone enough money to live all year. Promoters hold their shows in well-populated areas, in or around large cities. Advertising is good, and there is lots of it.

The *Hello Dolly* doll show is put on five or six times a year in Culver City, California by Arlene Adler and Mary Lou Admiston. They advertise in the free columns of doll magazines. Before each show, they send a post card to people who have attended in the past. The show has many excellent dealers and has had many years of success.

Some show promoters have added doll shows to their antiques, gun or ceramic promotional packages, such as Old Shoe Promotions and Bohler Promotions. Many shows are held in large convention halls. Today, many younger women successfully promote doll shows as a second job, and opportunities seem to be wide open in many sections of the country. When they first begin, some doll shows tie in with other shows, such as craft, miniatures, toys or antique shows.

Doll conventions held for large or small doll organizations can be a big event. Conventions are gatherings in which people come and stay while the show is being held—they must be housed, fed and entertained. Many conventions are filled almost as soon as advertising begins. The Doll Artisan Guild convention is an international one, and it is always filled early. Conventions are big business for promoters.

Left: Mary Queen of Scots, by Susan Cathey Dunham. This totally original 3-dimensional portrait doll is richly costumed in silk and velvet. See the "Dollionaire" story of Susan on page 117.

At doll shows and conventions, some of the biggest drawing cards are the exhibits and competitions. Competitions of reproduction dolls, artists' original dolls and antique dolls draw many people. Some people come to see their friends' dolls win blue ribbons, and often many become involved in the doll world. Exhibitors exhibit their dolls and often purchase materials for their next dolls.

Classes and seminars, held at shows and conventions by experts, also help bring in crowds. Usually people sign up in advance, and classes are full before the convention or show starts. Participants want to learn, as well as buy, and this helps make the show a success for promoters.

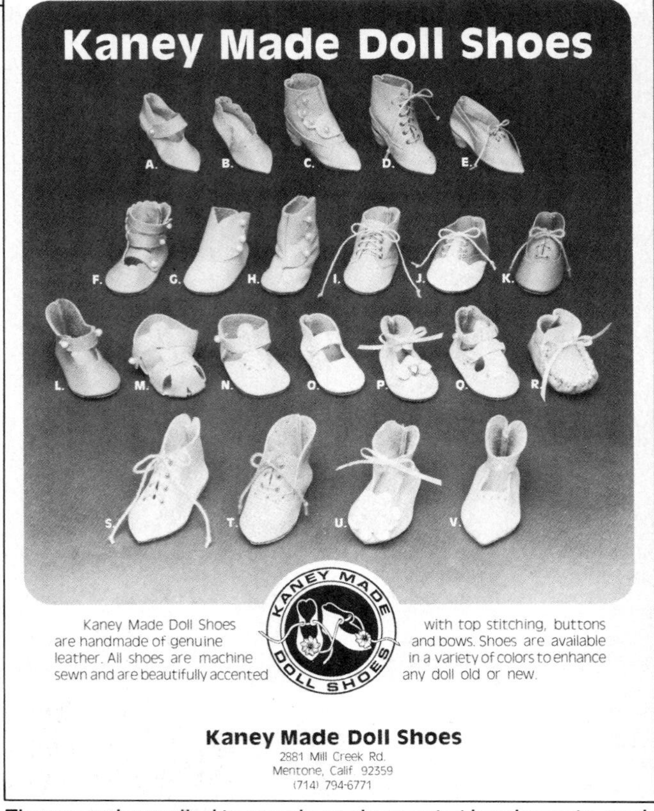

Flyers can be mailed to people or given out at local events, such as doll shows. Flyers can be very good for advertising your services or products.

MAKING YOURS A SUCCESSFUL DOLL SHOW

There are certain formulas for successful doll shows. Everything in a successful doll show hinges on two things—people to buy dolls and products to purchase.

- Advertise in doll magazines, through local or direct mail and by word-of-mouth.
- Find the right place to hold the show. It should have enough space and light, be air-conditioned or heated, have easy access for customers and provide adequate parking.
- Sell booth space at competitive prices. Provide enough tables and chairs for salespeople, and be sure there is a varied range of products.
- Have food available; it's another way to make money.
- A guest doll celebrity, competitive exhibits, donations of door prizes, prizes for the best sales booths, appraisals and free literature for other shows are optional, but they may help bring people to the doll show.

Who Runs a Doll Show?—A doll show can be run by doll-club members, doll organizations, individuals, families or professional promoters. Anyone or any organization can decide to hold a doll show. You don't need to be an expert, but you must be good at organization and pay attention to details. You need some original ideas and the ability to get along with people to put on a great doll show.

Selecting a Date—Pay special attention to selecting a date. The date should be decided from 6 months to 1 year in advance of the show. This is because doll dealers cover many shows and have their travel schedules set up well in advance.

When selecting a date, consider the weather in your area. It wouldn't be a good idea to hold a doll show in northern New Hampshire in midwinter when roads are icy or a big snowstorm could keep people from getting there. On the other hand, midwinter would be ideal for Florida or Arizona, which has delightful weather at that time of year. People love an excuse to visit winter holiday places when they can consider it a business trip.

Flyers are often colorful and attractive, such as this one by Dianne Dengel.

Just before a holiday or during a holiday season are good times so vacations can be planned around the show. Before Christmas is good just about anywhere to catch the Christmas trade.

If you're setting up a doll show that will be held every 3 months or so, let doll people know by handing out flyers, and get their cooperation in planning ahead for dates.

Where a Show Is Held—The place a doll show is held is very important. It must have enough space to hold the required number of booths that have preregistered. It should have wide aisles for easy movement. Try to include places for customers to sit. A show place must also have bathroom facilities.

The building must be easily accessible to customers and dealers who must bring in their wares. There must be plenty of parking. The building must be well-lighted and heated or cooled for the comfort of all.

Many of the very large doll shows are held in city convention centers or at fairgrounds. Large doll shows are also held in hotels. Smaller ones are held in women's clubs, YWCAs, legion halls, granges or even large studios. Provide tables and chairs or rent them where the show is held. In large shows, a loudspeaker system is necessary for announcing door-prize winners and for making announcements.

Many dolls are made each year as convention souvenirs. These two dolls, Pinky and Blue Boy, are souvenir dolls made by Linda Cheek.

There must be a convenient place for doll dealers to get a sandwich and a cup of coffee. If the show is held in a hotel or convention center, this is usually not a problem. If the show is in a club or grange, you may want to supply food as an extra money maker. Sometimes you can let another organization, such as a church group, use this as a money-raising project. At the last doll show I attended, the promoter provided cookies, punch and coffee for dealers and customers; customers stayed longer and may have purchased more.

DOLL CONVENTIONS

Doll conventions are usually held by doll groups or doll organizations. They are held over a period of days—anywhere from 2 to 6 days.

With a convention, interested people pay a fee in advance (sometimes more than a year in advance with regional conventions held by the UFDC). This fee does not include the hotel or meals. Conventions are a gathering of people who are interested in dolls for the purpose of promoting their particular doll interests. They pay for classes, workshops, entertainment and banquets in the advance fee. They serve as an audience for many doll-learning sessions, doll lectures, doll exhibits, workshops and salesroom for purchasing doll supplies.

Doll conventions take careful planning over a period of time and cooperation of all those involved. There are many doll conventions being held today, and each group or type of doll collected has its own. There are conventions for paper dolls, doll artists, doll makers, Ginnie Dolls, Drayton dolls—almost any type of doll has a convention built around it.

The best way to prepare to put on a doll convention is to attend several. Take notes of how they are run. Consult with people who put them on, and listen to their problems. Putting on a convention is a big undertaking, so start small.

To be successful, doll conventions must have a theme so doll people know in advance what value the convention will be to them. A doll club in Phoenix puts on what they call a "miniconvention." They have exhibits, workshops, a banquet and a lecture—all in one day, for one fee. It's like a taste of a major convention.

Conventions can make money for the clubs, organizations or people who put them on, if they are done correctly. Current advanced enrollment for a convention that lasts 3 to 5 days runs from $115 to $165. This does *not* include the hotel room or your meals. It usually includes a souvenir doll and a souvenir book.

HOW-TO SHOWS AND VIDEOTAPES

How-to Shows—The Public Broadcasting System (PBS) indicates that by public interest they realize more Americans are getting involved in do-it-yourself projects, such as making quilts, fixing the family car, learning photography and painting. So they run programs about these do-it-yourself projects. To the best of my knowledge, there is not a single series about doll making.

Judging by attendance at doll shows, doll making is one of the most popular hobbies today. I believe doll-making classes on educational television or a cable channel could pay off for a doll maker with ambition and knowledge.

Videotapes—There are two types of tapes made—the 1-inch tape, for broadcasting professionals, and home videotapes. At this time, I can count the instructive videotapes available to doll studios and doll makers on my fingers.

Production of videotapes is the newest way to make money in the field of dolls. For videotapes to be successful, the maker must know something the doll maker needs to know. He or she must be able to do the process better than the average doll maker and demonstrate it so it's interesting, precise and clear.

There is substantial cost in making tapes. Some people make them at home; other people use rented sound studios available at some universities and in larger cities. In addition to the cost of making the tape is the cost of *reproducing* it once a satisfactory tape is achieved, then *advertising* the finished product.

This is an untapped area of doll making. Attempt to make a tape *only* if you know something others need to know, if you can do something better, have a new angle or can show how to do something in a new way. This is a field where *only* the strong and the best will win.

Today, few videotapes are available that cover pouring doll molds and cleaning greenware, painting dolls, repairing antique dolls and modeling dolls.

Videotapes can also be rented or loaned to promote doll modeling seminars, costume classes, doll-painting classes or mold-making classes. Tapes can be used at conventions or doll shows and in doll shops. They can even be used at home.

Some tapes available at this time are listed on page 131, with addresses for ordering. Before deciding to go into tape making, view ones that are already on the market.

BOB AND JUNE BECKETT

Without a doubt, Beckett Originals owes its great success to the combined talents of Bob and June Beckett. They have been carving wood dolls since 1974. Some of their carved child and baby dolls have soft bodies, with only carved heads, hands and feet. Their newest child dolls are articulated all-wood.

June says, "The stimulus of our own inner feelings, added to the desires of collectors, has pushed us to work on improving our work and our designs. We know there are more than 1,000 individually produced Beckett dolls. Each doll is a statement of our impressions of the innocence and dearness of children. No hand-carved doll of ours will be exactly like the one made before it.

"We even design doll clothing. This is a must because each of our dolls is a total design—a combination of Bob's ideas and mine. An undressed doll, clothed by someone else, would immediately partake of their design and lose something of ours. However, if I made all the clothing, I'd lose much of my carving time. Our dolls would be even more limited in production than they are now. We are very fortunate to have Louise Brown, a mountain woman of the Tennessee Cumberland Plateau, as our seamstress. She uses her many years of shirt-factory experience to make our little dresses, overalls and doll bodies.

"The pressure of filling orders stifles some artists and gives incentive to others. We find a simple list of dolls, handled by mail and made to order, and other dolls of our choice, sold directly at shows or where we appear in person, fill our lives best. This gives us the opportunity to create and still have dolls to sell by mail.

"The year 1985 marked the 11th year of our doll making. Since 1978, we have made dolls on a full-time basis, as our sole source of income. I still have the creative joy of knowing this is what I really want to do today, and tomorrow, and the next day."

DOLL AUCTIONS

Mention the words "doll auction," and the large doll-auction houses that have come into being in the last 10 years immediately come to my mind. Before that, dolls were sold at auctions along with household goods, antiques or estate sales. Some international auction houses were already in business and merely added doll auctions.

Today, auctioning dolls is one of the most lucrative divisions of the doll industry. More is involved than just auctioning off someone's doll collection and collecting the 20 or 30% commission.

An auction company usually picks up dolls from the owner, catalogs them and insures them for safekeeping until the time of the auction. It's up to the auction company to present each doll at its best to get the highest price.

Many dolls must be photographed to be shown in an auction catalog. The catalog, with complete, accurate descriptions, is another essential part of selling by auction. Advertising and a suitable place to hold an auction are additional concerns and expenses.

Doll auction houses who sell only dolls, such as Cohen's and Theriault's, make their living this way. They must worry about having a collection to sell when they hold auctions. Finding 400 or more dolls to sell each month is *not* easy.

Mold makers are the highest-paid employees in the doll industry. Their craft demands talent and knowledge of many aspects of doll making.

More doll auctions are starting up. Some are small, and some are growing fast. This spreads even thinner the number of old dolls that can change hands. There are only so many antique dolls!

Other types of money-making auctions are also being held. One doll club I know made beautiful porcelain dolls representing children of different countries, then auctioned them off to raise money for a regional convention. The dolls were well-done, and the auction was a great success.

Another case I know about concerns a convention at which donated doll items (some of sentimental value, some of intrinsic value) were auctioned off. The money they raised was used for doll-making scholarships for young, energetic doll makers. An auction was also part of the UFDC convention in Atlanta in 1985.

A money-making auction was also held at a private doll show. It was a silent auction where people crossed off the last bid and put their own bid on a pad beside the doll. I hate to pass judgment on new ideas, but this was not considered (by bidders) to be a fair or successful type of auction.

A doll club was given an antique doll and auctioned it to help the club raise money for a regional convention. Members handed out or mailed to prospective buyers a description of the doll, along with a photograph and the page number of a doll price guide where the doll was listed with its current value. Recipients bid on the doll—I thought this was a novel idea, bid on the doll and was the highest bidder. I got the doll and have been well-satisfied.

There are some special qualifications needed by a person who is thinking of going into the doll auction business. First is integrity; it has always been the one thing in doll businesses that has set the winners apart. A good rapport with doll collectors is essential. I would also add enthusiasm to these qualifications.

MONEY FROM MOLD MAKING

In the world of ceramics and dolls, a mold maker is one of the highest-paid professionals, and he is paid according to his skill. A *mold maker* is the person who makes the first (original) mold of a doll or object. He is *not* the person who pours plaster into cases to reproduce a mold. That person needs very little skill.

A skilled mold maker who works for a large corporation that makes molds of dolls is often financially well off. Mold makers for ceramic companies make top salaries.

Mold-making skills can be used in many ways to make money. Below is a list of some ways I have seen mold making used.

1. Make molds of an artist's original dolls.
2. Make commercial molds for artists who wish to sell molds.
3. Make molds for convention dolls. (Each year many doll conventions are held; some use a doll as a favor or door prize.)
4. Make molds of antique dolls to sell.

5. Get a job with a doll company as a mold maker.
6. Make molds of doll accessories, such as doll dishes, small cradles or beds.
7. Make molds for an original-doll series.
8. Make molds for the production of felt dolls. Felt and fabric dolls, with shaped faces, are pressed in molds.
9. Make body molds from antique doll bodies.
10. Make original doll-body molds to fit original or reproduction dolls.
11. Make molds of antique-doll hands and feet to replace broken ones. (I know of two people who have become successful selling replacement parts for dolls.)
12. Make molds of china hands and feet.
13. Make molds of rare, antique china dolls—few molds of this type are available on the market.
14. Teach mold making to classes who make dolls and to people who wish to become mold makers.

The skill of the mold maker is not an inborn trait but something that can be learned. It can be learned by most people in a week of lessons (sometimes 3 days), depending on the ability of the instructor to teach and make good molds.

Some people teach mold making to a group who is interested only in making one mold of their own modeled doll head. Lewis Goldstein teaches a simplified method of mold making. He is listed on page 124.

You will have to search to find mold makers who will teach you their skills. Some retired mold makers may teach one person, or a few people, at a time. Be prepared to pay a good price when you ask a mold maker to teach you what he has spent a lifetime learning.

Mold making, especially of dolls, is a specialized skill that can be learned. Some master mold makers are willing to teach others the craft of making molds.

COSTUMING

Costuming dolls is one of the best ways to make money in the doll world today. At the top of the list is the doll couturier, who makes the finest handsewn French costumes. A doll costumer who understands fine pleating, draping and fitting can command a high price for any costume she makes.

If you're interested in creating costumes, all done with fine French handsewing, this is another area to explore. Making these costumes is often so time-consuming that most profit is lost. These fine dresses are covered in lace, with intricate detail work. For more information on costuming, read my book *Doll Costuming*, also published by HPBooks.

There is also a market for play costumes for German character dolls (most are children). The original costumes of these dolls were made of such poor material that most of the old costumes have disintegrated.

Exact reproduction of an old costumes is always in demand because few seamstresses are accurate enough in style and construction to create them. I am still trying to find someone to whom I can say, "Please copy this antique outfit," who will do it accurately with old material I

Above: John and Pat Garretson had a booth at a doll show presenting Heirloom Creations. These dresses represent hours of French handsewing and smocking.

Right: Jackie Jones has reached the pinnacle of doll costuming. She was a hat designer for women in Chicago; today she makes hats and costumes for French dolls.

supply. Many seamstresses are artists and prefer to do their own thing.

Bonnets and Hats—There is also good money in crocheting bonnets for baby dolls and young-child dolls in the old patterns with old ribbon decorations.

Some hat makers in this country can make hats similar to French doll hats made 100 years ago. These people command high prices for their work and cannot make enough hats to keep up with the demand. Making hats takes skill; they are made by winding straw braid, gathering material to the brim and attaching lining and decorations.

Other hats with tasteful trim for less-expensive dolls are also in demand. Boy hats and character hats for German dolls are always desired.

Fabrics and Materials—Antique materials to make costumes for antique dolls is always in demand and brings a high price. Materials must be purchased from all over the world. Fabrics must be suitable for dolls and sturdy enough to last at least 10 years.

You may have some difficulty selling old materials after you locate them because people want to see the actual fabrics and are hesitant to order through the mail. It might be wise to sell old materials at doll shows or conventions.

Along with old materials, there is a demand for trim. Fine old laces, in different types and widths, old tatting and crocheted edgings are always sought by collectors of old dolls.

Old materials to make socks and stockings is also important. Socks and stockings were one of the first things to disintegrate or be lost, so they must often be replaced on an old doll.

Think of the number of hats, bonnets, dresses, baby gowns, underclothing and stockings that must be made for reproduction and limited-edition dolls that are being made. Most doll artists are not seamstresses and must ask someone to dress their dolls. Maybe this is a need you can fill.

Seamstresses make more money by working for a company that produces a very special limited-edition doll or by working for several reproduction artists that provide steady work.

One couple I know makes lace-trimmed silk dresses for dolls in many sizes. They sell the costumes they make at conventions and through catalogs.

Some dealers display racks of dresses at conventions, with dresses from different seamstresses. Others sell costumes on consignment. (Consignment selling is usually a poor practice and is discussed on page 34.)

Shoes—Shoemaking is a field in itself. Some doll shoemakers have made a good living for many years producing shoes for dolls. Shoes often cost as much, or more, than a pair of children's shoes. This is still a good field to get into, even though many people now make doll shoes. Design, skill and ingenuity are needed to accurately reproduce old shoes.

Making and selling shoe patterns is good to a certain extent. Many doll makers make their own doll shoes and want to purchase only the patterns. These patterns may be produced more profitably if they are included with an article about old doll shoes for a magazine.

Pattern Making—Pattern making is another skill that has been profitable. Skill in pattern design, knowing how to write easy-to-follow directions and professional printing is necessary to make a success of pattern making.

Today, only a few good patterns for authentic French costumes are available. There are thousands of poorly made patterns on the market—including some of my own. Pattern making is a precise art. If you can make patterns, and make them right, it might be your end of the rainbow. Patterns cost little to produce or ship; the main cost is advertising.

OLD-DOLL SEMINARS

Seminars on antique dolls and old dolls, and information about collecting are relatively new to the doll scene. I have been giving these types of seminars in my home, using my own doll collection, for some time. I usually do it for a doll club.

These seminars are all types and sizes—from the 1-hour lecture with a single speaker to the 2-day, multispeaker gathering.

Pat Gosh held one of these seminars at UCLA—it was the most complete, most intensive and, probably, the best I have attended. She covered the structure of different types of dolls and how to select artist dolls, German dolls, French dolls and composition dolls for a collection.

Pat carefully selected her speakers and illustrative materials, and she put together a fine exhibit of dolls to illustrate every point. The seminar ran one day, from 9 a.m. to 5 p.m., with a short break for lunch. It was well-attended and cost $90 per person. Everyone I talked to felt it was worth the trip, the time and the cost.

George and Florence Theriault hold seminars all over the country in connection with their auctions. Because they handle so many dolls, they have firsthand knowledge others do not have. They are both good speakers and tell the doll story as they see it, holding back nothing. Seminars I have attended are stimulating, informative and interesting. The cost of seminars varies in price, depending on how long it is.

In the state of Washington, Doll Club Study Seminars set up a series of 10 sessions (10 sessions running between 8:30 and 5:30), all on the same day. The classes dealt with cloth dolls, teddy bears, German character, French dolls, Lencis, Schoenhuts, chinas and primitives. Classes were priced $15 *per* session. The seminar was run in connection with an appraisal clinic and a doll show held by the same group on the following day.

Some UFDC doll clubs are study clubs and spend their meeting time researching dolls. This accomplishes the same thing as some old-doll seminars on a smaller scale.

We need more educational doll classes. The more we know about dolls, the more we can experience the fun of collecting. If you're thinking of planning a seminar, try to attend some *before* you make your final plans.

DOLL APPRAISALS

Doll appraising isn't a full-time business, but it can make an interesting side job. If you're already into dolls, doing appraisals can be an extra service you offer. Doll appraisal is good for an antique-doll shop owner, an antique-doll seller who has no shop or a person who loves to spend the weekend at doll shows. Many auctioneers are also doll appraisers. I appraise dolls in my home—more for the fun of it than anything.

A doll-show promoter loves to have a doll appraiser there because it brings more people to the show. Many people who come in with a doll to be appraised will also purchase new shoes, a wig or whatever the doll needs. The fact that a doll appraiser will be present and the cost of appraising each doll should appear in literature advertising the show so people will bring their dolls with them to the show.

Fees and the completeness of an appraisal vary. Written appraisals, filling out a page similar to the form shown on page 106, usually cost $10 to $15. Verbal appraisals of two or three dolls is usually $10, but this can vary. At these prices, the appraisal is just a service.

To qualify as a doll appraiser, you must be able to recognize dolls and markings at a glance. You must also know the history of many different dolls, approximate dates dolls were made and up-to-the-minute selling prices. You must be able to back up your statements with auction books, doll-history books and price guides. Even the best doll appraiser occasionally gets a doll she doesn't know. Say you don't know the doll, then find a doll as near as possible to it in a price guide for appraisal purposes.

Most doll appraisers leave some leeway in their pricing. They give the price as a range, such as $300 to $350. The more valuable the doll is, the more leeway they leave themselves. For example, with a Jumeau they might say from $3,000 to $3,500.

COLLECTION APPRAISALS

Many people with large collections want to have all their dolls appraised at the same time. This type of appraisal creates new arrangements. To do the job properly, an appraiser must set aside several hours, a whole day or, with a very large collection, perhaps several days.

A doll collection may be in another city or another state. You may have travel and hotel expenses. You'll have to figure these costs, plus the appraisal of the number of dolls, ahead of time. Usually people want to know how much it will cost *before* they hire anyone for the job. Some doll appraisers work by the hour on large collections. They get $50 and up per hour, plus expenses. Some charge as much as $200 an hour.

Don't set yourself up as a doll appraiser unless you are qualified. Too many people advertise they are doll appraisers, but they have few qualifications for the job.

To become a qualified doll appraiser takes years of study, comparison and actually working with dolls. I know people who claim to be appraisers who aren't; I wouldn't let them touch a good doll. When choosing an appraiser, I tell people they must have confidence the appraiser can handle the dolls and believe the appraiser has a good knowledge of doll values.

Licensing doll appraisers is not required under any state laws. Some people who are qualified to appraise bisque or china dolls have no knowledge of composition dolls. If you are hiring an appraiser, ask for references of people whose dolls he or she has appraised.

It's better not to sell your dolls to an appraiser because he'll be setting his own price on your dolls. It is unethical for a person appraising a collection to offer to buy a doll from the collection. On the other hand, many times dealers will give a price on an entire collection, and if it is satisfactory, the collection is sold. This is different because the owner of the collection and the dealer have this in mind from the start of the arrangement.

There are many reasons for having a collection appraised. Whatever your reason for having an appraisal, choose the appraiser carefully.

- Dolls over $300 usually must be appraised, including a written document, for insurance purposes.
- A collection of dolls that spans a lifetime has changed in value so dramatically in the last 10 years that an owner needs to know their value.
- A doll collection may be inherited, and the

XAVIER ROBERTS

The designer of the Cabbage Patch Kids, Xavier Roberts, became a millionaire before he was 30. Many doll businesses have tried to ignore the whole Cabbage Patch occurrence, but they really wish they were clever enough to come up with the successful formula for advertising that Appalachian Art Works and Coleco used to make their Cabbage Patch Kids so popular and well-known.

No one questions the fact that advertising worked. Few dolls have had the television exposure Cabbage Patch dolls have had—much of it during the time children watch TV. There has been a lot of advertising in magazines and newspapers—almost any magazine you pick up has Cabbage Patch Kids. Some ads are full color or full pages with good, catchy phrases.

Besides skillful advertising, Coleco presented over 250 related products to go with the Cabbage Patch Kids. The adoption idea, braces for toothless dolls, names for dolls, birth certificates and even 5-1/2- and 3-1/2-inch dolls in vending machines are all part of the strategy of this business phenomenon.

To further publicize what has happened, there is now a book, *Fantasy, The Incredible Cabbage Patch Phenomenon*, by William Hoffman. Study what has happened with Cabbage Patch dolls. Advertising has been appealing, creative and abundant—this is what has given rise to the millions of Cabbage Patch dolls. And it all started with Roberts and one sewing machine.

new owner wants to know what she has received.

- A doll collection is to be sold by the owner, and she needs an outside opinion on the value of the dolls.

Some family dolls are more valuable than their owners had expected. Other dolls, such as plain chinas, have increased little in value.

Owners must be aware of the different prices on a single doll. The *retail* price of the doll is the value given by the appraiser. If you are going to insure the doll, the retail price is the *replacement price*. There is also the *dealer's price*, which is what a dealer can pay you and still mark up the doll and make a profit. A dealer will offer about 30% less than the retail price. There is still another, lower price. This is the price you get if you sell the doll as *part of a collection* that contains excellent and poor dolls.

If you explore doll appraising, keeping in mind the appraiser and owner and see both sides, you may be able to make improvements in your services. The better you are as an appraiser, the higher fee you can command.

DOLL APPRAISAL BY MAIL

Another service in great demand is doll appraisals for people who live far from doll shops or doll auctions. These people have dolls they want identified—they want some history on the doll and perhaps its value. This is not an easy thing to do from photographs. It's time consuming to look up dolls and be accurate as to dates and data. I don't make a practice of identifying and appraising dolls from descriptions and photographs, but I do get asked for help from people who don't know where else to turn for information.

If you want to do this as part of a business, create a form that has specific questions to ask to gather as much information as possible. You also need to ask for three photos—full doll, front, undressed; closeup of face front; photo of any markings. (These are not always possible.)

You must tell the person seeking the information that this type of appraisal cannot be as accurate as an in-person appraisal because it's easy to leave out some very important fact, such as as a hairline crack or an eye chip.

Below is a sample form I have developed. It asks many pertinent questions. Use this form as it is, or use it to create your own form.

Doll Appraisal Form

1. Doll height ________________________________
2. Doll markings on back of head, in order, as they appear on doll
____
____
____
3. Doll's head is (check one)
( ) bisque ( ) composition ( ) china, shiny ( ) papier-mâché ( ) other
4. Body markings, if any ________________________________
____
5. Eyes are (check one)
( ) glass, paperweight ( ) glass, sleep eyes ( ) painted ( ) other
6. Condition of wig (check one) ( ) poor ( ) fair ( ) excellent
7. Describe any cracks or damage to head or eyes ________________________________
____
8. Condition of body (check one) ( ) fair ( ) good ( ) excellent
9. Is there any eye shadow over eyes? ( ) yes ( ) no
10. Is the mouth open or closed? ________________________________
11. Does doll have teeth? ________________________________
12. Did clothing come with doll? ________________________________
Check whether it was ( ) original ( ) mothermade ( ) new
13. Markings from bottom of shoes, if any ________________________________
____
14. Give any known dates, or approximate, dates you have on doll
____
____
15. Additional description, if necessary ________________________________
____
____
____
____

BARBARA ELMORE

Sometimes you meet someone who is just entering the doll world, and you can predict his or her success. This happened with Barbara Elmore; she had ambition and talent to paint and create designs from dolls. Today, Barbara paints canvases for needlepoint workers. She paints dolls with character and light in their eyes. She has been engaged by a company as their designer for a new doll fabric item. When you meet someone with this kind of talent, you know they are "dollionaires" of the future.

DOLLS IN THE UNIVERSITY OR COLLEGE

In the last few years, many doll classes and symposiums have been held at universities. These are usually special sessions under the Extension Service or the Art Department. Some universities include courses on doll making in their costume section of Home Economics. A few schools have added work on costuming or making dolls for senior-citizen, non-credit courses.

Colleges and universities are slow to add something new, but this is a good place for a qualified doll teacher to work into a good salaried position.

Many events and classes have also been held. UCLA ran an all-day seminar for the interested public in June, 1985. The seminar cost $90 and ran from 8:30 to 5:00; Pat Gosh ran the well-attended event.

Dottie Baker has taught a course on the History of Dolls at Santa Monica Community College for over 6 years. Classes are offered under Community Services, and anyone can register for them. Each class runs 9 hours—in three 3-hour sessions. It costs $25 for each class, and there are usually about 20 to 25 students in each class.

Early in 1985, the Art Department of Northern Illinois University at DeKalb held a doll display that lasted for almost a month. Three rooms were set up with dolls to illustrate fashions of the 1800s, and over 200 dolls were exhibited. The display, done by the Illinois-Wisconsin Doll Club, the University Art Department and the Illinois Arts Council, was well-attended.

At Meridith College, in Raleigh, North Carolina, a Doll Symposium is held each year in June. This is sponsored by the Office of Continuing Education. In its first year, 1981, they had a registration of 700 interested doll lovers. Each year has brought a larger registration.

DOLLS AS A PART OF ADVERTISING

Many large companies use dolls as premiums. This has been going on for over 100 years. In 1911, Daisy, a bisque-headed doll, was offered as a premium by *Ladies Home Journal* for a predetermined number of subscriptions.

Some people use their shopping bags for advertising, such as these bags by Theriault and Janice Naibert.

Lithographed patterns on cloth to be made into Aunt Jemima, Uncle Moe, Wade and Diana dolls were made from 1908 to 1925 and sold for 25 cents, plus an Aunt Jemima flour box top.

In 1916, T. Babbitt Cleanser contracted with Modern Toy Co. to make a 15-inch "Babbitt, at Your Service Cleanser Boy." The William Wrigley Co. advertised the Spearmint Kid in 1915, which sold for $1.

From 1920 to 1925, Buddy Lee dolls were made and dressed in denim overalls to advertise the H.D. Lee Mercantile Co., which was a manufacturer of overalls.

The Campbell Kids were first made in 1910 by Horsmann for the Joseph Campbell Co. In 1895, Northwestern Consolidated Milling Co. began using their farm-boy trademark; the doll had Ceresota Flour printed on his chest.

In 1910, Naptha Soap Powder gave away a doll when the customer sent in a certain number of coupons from the soap box. The doll was called the Cinderella Doll.

A likeness-doll, representing Douglas Fairbanks in the film *The Thief of Bagdad,* was made in 1924 to advertise the film. I have no count on the number of advertising dolls that were done to advertise Shirley Temple movies.

Today, Rose Tea has a miniature doll, Puffy Pops-Rite has a fabric doll, Nabisco offers a fabric doll, Charlie Tuna has a plush doll, Kraft has a puppet, Elmer's Glue has doll-house plans and General Foods has a cardboard bake shop. These are only a few of the many companies that use dolls and doll items as premiums.

It might be interesting to make a study of how many advertising dolls are in doll collections today. It will give you and others a background in what has been done; this might inspire you or others as doll makers to approach today's companies about making dolls and doll items for them. All these dolls (and those to come) were designed and made by a doll artist. This might be another type of job you might try.

ORGANIZATION DOLLS

Look for jobs, or make jobs for yourself. You must see the possibilities of a job and present the idea to any large or small organization. Organizations, such as the Shriners, Girl Scouts, the military, ball teams—any organization that has a uniform or something special in the way of clothing or hats, could possibly need a doll. Make dolls for these organizations to sell as a money maker or for their own members to purchase.

Make up a doll with the uniform of the organization you wish to approach. Work out your costs and time schedule, then present the idea, along with the doll, to the president of the organization. The doll must be sold at a price so the organization makes money, so price your dolls wholesale, by the dozen or hundred. If you get an order, buy your materials wholesale, and use production methods to produce the quantity ordered.

DOLL SERVICES

Study what is on the market today; study magazine and newspaper advertising to see if you can come up with a doll idea that would fit a particular company. Then make an appointment with the president of the company. This can be done by a letter that briefly describes your idea and photos that show the quality of your work. Sometimes, but not always, the entire project can be set in motion over the telephone.

Several months ago I had a meeting with Barbara Elmore. She desperately wanted to get a doll-painting job. Through my encouragement, she has tried several avenues. It finally all came together for her after she sent some photos of her work to a company I recommended. Now her work will be mass produced, and she will earn a royalty for her work.

COSTUMES

When the Ice Capades first started, the company purchased dolls and had them costumed in outfits they intended to use in the show. This was a big time-saver because the costume was designed first in miniature. It was an economical way to test the costume because little material was needed for the doll costumes. It gave the producers a chance to see the costumes together and to judge their color and usability. Everyone wanted to buy the dolls, so later dolls were made and sold wearing the costumes.

The same thing happened with the Rockettes in Radio City. Many children who saw the Rockettes wanted a doll in their likeness to take home. Someone had to design and produce these dolls.

CHURCH GROUPS

Churches often struggle for money. It is possible a church could appeal to its members for dolls, and, as a dealer, you could purchase any donated dolls. This could make the church a substantial amount of money from these "doll gifts." The person arranging this must have substantial knowledge of dolls so it is fair to everyone. I believe a second opinion or an outside appraisal in this situation might be called for.

One unique situation I know of is carried out by a Catholic priest named Fr. Crandall. His parish is in Worchester, New York, which is a small town. Fr. Crandall goes to France to buy dolls, then sells them at his church for a profit.

This child's simple pleated silk dress was sold by Countess Marie Tarnowska for $140. Making reproduction costumes for French bébé dolls is a very popular business for many people.

IDEAS FOR PRODUCING DOLLS IN COSTUMES

Use the following list to help you generate some ideas for yourself. There may be many other occupations or organizations you could make dolls for.

- Industries
- Professions
- Business
- Celebrities
- Holiday characters
- Religious groups
- Teachers
- Celebrities
- Cowboys
- Fishermen
- Lumberjacks
- Butchers
- Seamstresses
- Clowns
- Doll makers
- Cooks
- Priests
- Nuns
- Astronauts

FOLK-ART DOLLS

Folk-art dolls, or craft dolls, are American. There is no age or cut-off date for folk-art dolls. These dolls are simple and made of materials at hand; many are still being made and sold. More interest is being given to this type of doll. Often these dolls are made by Appalachian mountain people to supplement their incomes, but dolls are not limited to that area. Dolls are made of common materials, without a great deal of work, and most sell for under $100.

Another idea that goes along with folk-art dolls *of the past* is the true reproduction of antique folk-art dolls. Little has been done here. An Izanna Walker folk-art doll sold for $14,000 at a 1984 auction, which shows there is room for reproduction dolls in this area. Painting on Walker dolls was exquisite, and it will take a true doll artist to reproduce them in the quality of workmanship that was originally used.

There are other folk-art dolls, such as dolls by Emma Adams, Drayton and Beecher that could be copied. Being able to purchase true reproduction folk-art dolls would make many doll collectors who cannot pay the price of an original very happy, and it would make money for you as a doll maker.

SERVICES

Below is a list of doll services I have compiled—think about all the needs waiting to be filled. Look around your area, study magazines on dolls and talk to other people. You'll probably be able to think of other services that fill a definite need.

Custom-made wigs for dolls
Doll Christmas decorations
Doll appraisals by mail or in person
Doll vocabularies that can be copied for doll-making lessons
Doll-making lessons that can be copied for students
Doll-show judging sheets that can be duplicated
Judging at doll shows
Lectures on antique dolls
Making original mechanical dolls
Painted portraits of real children and their dolls
Photo or painting of customer and favorite doll
Photography of dolls for security and insurance purposes
Portrait dolls from photos of real children
Portrait dolls in felt, porcelain, stockinette, wood
Programs on dolls showing part of a collection
Reconditioning of old doll bodies
Reconditioning of old doll wigs
Repairing bisque heads
Repairing composition bodies
Repairing modern dolls
Repairing old mechanical dolls
Seminars on old dolls
Stringing old and new dolls
Teaching charts and models for studios
Videocassette programs on dolls
Workshops on dolls—making, repairing, costuming, cleaning

One of Sue Solomon's miniature dolls.

VIRGINIA LaLORGNA

Virginia LaLorgna contributes her success in the world of reproduction dolls to her creation of *authentic* reproductions. She was a 1984 Millie winner for her exquisite painting of fine reproduction dolls.

SUE MAHURIN

Sue Mahurin designs clothes, her first love, and makes miniature dolls, her second love. She has a wonderful time painting the dolls' faces and styling their hair. She makes all accessories—shoes, hats, parasols, muffs and jewelry. She treasures working at home doing something that is creative and rewarding.

Working with dolls is more fun for Sue than any other kind of work. The three main inspirations in Sue's life were the Thorn Miniature rooms in the Art Institute in Chicago, Colleen Moore's Doll House in the Museum of Science and Industry, also in Chicago, and beautiful scraps of fabric given to Sue as a child by her aunt, a dressmaker.

Sue worked at designing—first telephone displays, then sportswear for a bra company, then assistant dress designer for Blevins Vogue. With three small children to take care of, she also did custom dressmaking in her home. Then she changed careers and enrolled at John Marshall Law School in Chicago. She studied law for a while, then became a real-estate broker.

"I found I loved old houses. I bought several large, old homes, saw to remodeling and decorating, then sold them." Sue says, "It was like playing with doll houses, only they were full size." She painted and made felt murals, then took up writing. She has written four gothic mystery novels and has 11 more outlined.

Today, what has brought all her loves together is the purchase of three doll houses that were incomplete until she made the doll-house dolls to go in them. They were such fun to make, and everyone wanted to buy her dolls—now, Sue does nothing but dolls. Like many of us, Sue experimented with careers until she found her place—with dolls!

Writing Opportunities

Success may be close at hand for talented writers—success may come in the form of good feelings or the reward of giving something of yourself to the world. Financial success in writing comes from best sellers, and only a few people will ever be successful in that way.

To be even moderately successful, a writer must have *discovered something, invented something, have a new angle, have new information* or *have an idea* to inspire readers. A writer will never be a success if he steals ideas or rehashes ideas from other books or works. A writer must work from his own experiences, knowledge and dreams.

When I write an article or book, I try to keep in mind the following ideas to help me organize my thoughts and my material.

1. To get something published, think of your audience—who will be reading this material? What you write must appeal, educate, give pleasure or stimulate a particular audience. Write at a level your audience will understand.
2. Your subject matter and its delivery must be meaningful to your audience. Study the publication in which you wish to have an article published, and be familiar with the type of material they regularly use.
3. You must know something others don't know—some new angle or new method—to write an article or book others will read.
4. Every time an antique doll is taken apart, something new is discovered about the way a doll is assembled or marked or the way a mold was made. This often lends itself to an article for a magazine.

Doll magazines often need well-written doll articles with good photographs. Small newsletters and small magazines may also publish an article, without paying for it, that will help boost your reputation.

Doll articles for magazines, newspapers and newsletters, other than those written on dolls, are acceptable. Articles on doll furniture, doll eyes or doll shoes are also good subjects to cover.

Left: Fine silks and silk taffeta, like this costume, are from imported fabrics. Fabrics and trims may make up the bulk of a business or just part of one, as is the case with Janice Naibert or Martha Watkins. Doll costumers must have the finest materials. This doll is leather-bodied F.G.

Finished dresses can be purchased in any size at a large doll show. These costumes are by Deja Vu Originals and Designs.

To create opportunities to make money with dolls in publishing, think about starting your own magazine or newsletter on dolls. How about writing a how-to book on felt or cloth dolls? Consider writing a factbook on various dolls, with many pictures. You might consider helping with doll-convention books; many doll conventions publish a souvenir book. Write how-to directions for making folk dolls.

Write about your experiences with dolls or doll making. Most doll makers have experienced joy, suffering, fun, drama, tragedy, excitement and inspiration. Every angle in doll making has its ups and downs and might make an interesting article.

Besides books and magazine articles, other areas to consider include price guides, directories, encyclopedias and repair books.

GENERAL INFORMATION FOR WRITERS

Below is a checklist I use to be sure everything I write is the best I can make it. Use any of the ideas on this list that will help you.

1. Draw up a comprehensive, clear outline *before* you begin to write. Work strictly from the outline.
2. Type material on good-quality paper, and type only on one side.
3. Double space and indent all paragraphs. Use wide margins.
4. Number each page in the upper-right corner.
5. Be sure punctuation, spelling and sentence structure are correct.
6. Underline or mark words that are to be set in italics or capitals.
7. Doublecheck all dates, names and addresses. Be sure they're correct!
8. Use headings.
9. Use your outline to help you create a good table of contents.
10. Proofread very carefully, and make any corrections *before* material leaves your hands.
11. Type your name and the title of the book or article on a cover sheet.
12. Write captions for illustrations on a separate sheet.
13. Make a carbon copy or photocopy, and send the original to the publisher.

Many publishers have definite ways they wish a manuscript to be prepared for submission. Before you do an entire manuscript, check with the publisher—it will save you time and money.

SUBMITTING WORK

If you wish to submit your work to a publisher, first write a letter of inquiry to see if they are interested in what you wish to write about. You may also assume they are interested by other books they have on the market.

Before you submit your book to a publishing company, send them:

- A letter briefly describing your background and other books you have published, who will buy your book, a discussion of competitive books and an explanation as to why you think your book should be published.
- A complete outline of the proposed material.
- Sample chapters.
- Sample photos and illustrations.

Keep copies of what you send. If you wish to submit short articles to magazines, send the complete article with illustrations or photos.

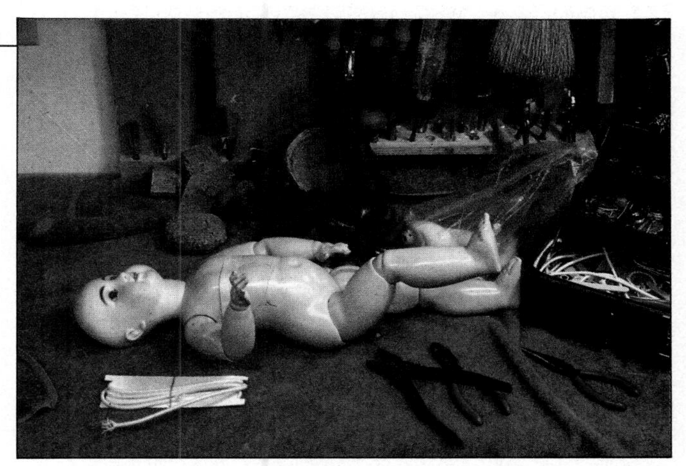

Doll repair is good business if done correctly. It is in great demand for antique dolls and could be an interesting topic for a book.

HOW TO GET PUBLISHED

There are three ways to get your book in print. You should understand how each system works before you get involved in any one.

Publishers—There are book publishers all over the country. Many are specialty publishers and publish a certain kind of book. They accept or reject proposed manuscripts from letters and portions of manuscripts that are submitted to them.

Publishers want to find people who are capable of writing books that sell well. If your book is accepted, the publishing company may pay you an advance against your royalties to help you while you are writing the book or to pay for photographs or illustrations. Royalties, minus the advance, are paid as books are sold. The publisher pays the cost of printing, promoting and advertising the book. Many publishers help with expenses when you promote the book.

Vanity Press—Unless you have been trying to get a book published, you may not be aware of vanity presses. These companies advertise they will publish your book—just send your manuscript, and they will evaluate it. These are usually *printers* that will print your book, and *you* pay for it. You end up with boxes of books on your doorstep and a big bill. People who have tried to get a book accepted by a regular publisher may, as a last resort, seek the services of a vanity publisher. I know of no instance where it has had a happy ending.

Self-Publishing—Some people have turned to self-publishing. You hire the printer, do the layout yourself and make all the decisions. You pay for the printing. You pay for the entire publishing operation yourself. This may work if you have a way of distributing and selling your books nationally. Can you imagine having the extra bedroom filled with boxes of books—thousands of them—and no planned way to sell them? There are several self-published books on the market now that are doing well, such as the book *Chinas, Dolls for Study and Admiration* by Mona Borger, Borger Publications. Mona Borger publishes her own books and sells them by advertising in all the doll magazines. All profit from the books is also hers.

To self-publish, you must have the money to pay for your illustrations, your time and the cost of printing the book. An 80-page book with color photos printed in runs of 5,000 could cost $25,000, not counting distribution costs. Full-page color separations for color pages can cost over $100 each just for separations.

There are many reasons for self-publishing. I used this method on my first two books because Vernon and I were selling doll molds, and doll makers needed instructions to go with the molds. We had a successful, established company and the national advertising necessary to sell the books. It was a very successful venture for us.

Some people, and their companies, have become successful publishers of doll books, such as Gary Rudell of Hobby House Press. Success could happen to you if you start out self-publishing, then expand to become a regular publisher.

If you're looking for a publisher of how-to books on dolls or a related subject, a doll company that sells materials you use and describe might be interested in publishing your book. Contact them about a joint venture.

For more information on potential publishers, go to the library and ask for the *LMP—Literary Market Place*. This volume is put out yearly and lists the name and address of almost every publisher in the United States. It also lists what types of books they publish. There's nothing worse than sending your manuscript on dolls to a publisher who's totally uninterested in publishing that kind of material. It wastes your time and money to send your material to the wrong publishing house.

If you have written something you believe is worth putting on the market, be persistent. Keep working at it until you get it published. Don't give up too quickly or easily!

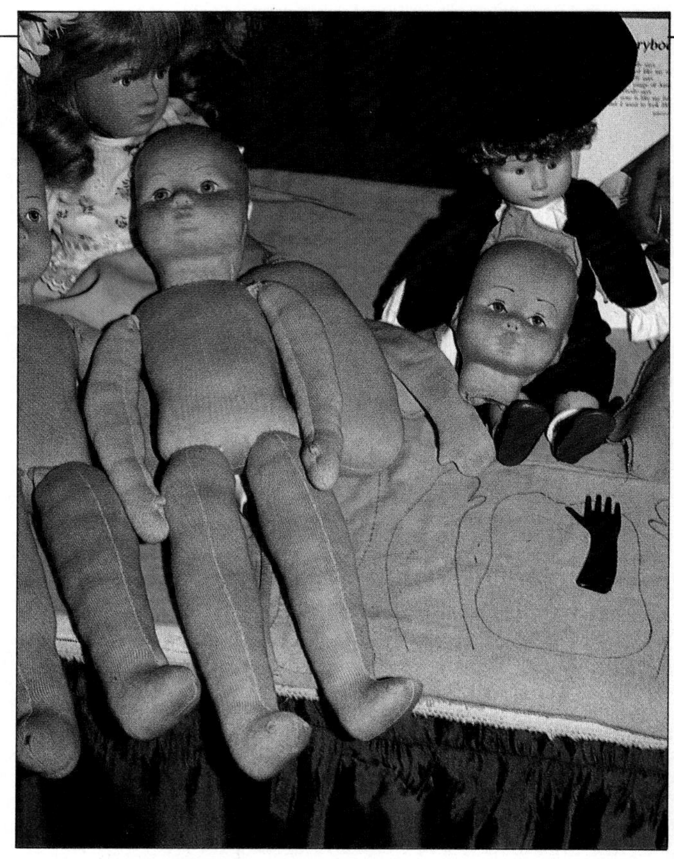

Above, right and far right: Maueshan Dolls makes and sells kits for doll parts imported from Switzerland. These are cotton tricot-type dolls currently sold in Neiman Marcus, Rardstroms and Knotts Berry Farm. Writing an article about unusual dolls like these might be a good way to start your writing career.

WHAT TO WRITE?

Below is a list of some things you might consider writing if this is an area you are very interested in.

American dolls and doll makers
Articles about today's doll artists
Books on doll care
Books on old dolls
Directions on doll repair
Directories of doll-accessory sellers
Directory of antique-doll sellers
Directory of doll makers
Directory of doll shops
Doll history
Doll newspaper on dolls
Doll-house articles
How to make anything connected with dolls
Instruction sheets for felt dolls or cloth dolls for magazines
Lesson plans for studios
Magazine articles
Newsletters
Price guides for doll furniture
Price guides for dolls
Question-and-answer columns for doll magazines
Research of doll makers
Teaching aids
Trade publications

SUSAN DUNHAM

"*Fantastic*" is how Susan Dunham describes her introduction to doll making in 1977. Susan had been painting portraits in oils and china painting when a friend convinced her to make a doll for fun. It was love from the very beginning.

For Susan, learning to make dolls in porcelain was difficult in rural Oregon in 1977 because supplies and lessons were not available. Susan forged on independently with the aid of one of my books. After several years of making antique replicas, Susan began to make original dolls. The first was made from modeling wax purchased at a local store. She taught herself, without instruction, to sculpt, design and make complicated molds, to make master molds and to do many other chores connected with making an original doll. Orders for her original dolls grew in number; extra hands were required to keep up.

Carefully selected people from the community were trained and incorporated into the growing business, which was called *Dunham Arts.* A new 1,600 square foot building was erected to house the doll-making business and the large collection of antique and new dolls Susan was adding.

In the large exhibit area, Susan has added French antique furniture and children's antique toys help to create the dreamland atmosphere of her soon-to-be museum. To date, she has created 35 different models of all types of dolls, and she remains dedicated to making the finest dolls in the world. See a photo of Susan's Mary Queen of Scots doll on page 94.

Additional Information to Help You

It's important for anyone involved with dolls to have the most complete, comprehensive guide to finding the information they seek. This section is devoted entirely to that end. I have drawn together all my resources to compile these lists. My goal has been to pull together *everything* I have access to that could help you in some way. I hope the books, magazines, names, addresses and various other information supplied here will help you in some way.

BOOKS AND MAGAZINES

There are many sources of information about dolls. Magazines, price guides and resource books help keep you abreast of what is happening in the doll world. Below is a fairly complete list of books and magazines *anyone* involved with dolls may be able to use. Whether you are interested in dolls for collecting purposes and enjoyment or as part of your business, these publications will help you in many ways.

Some of the material is in the form of newsletters and pamphlets. It will take some hunting on your part to find them because many are not readily available. If you have any problems locating what you want, ask your local librarian for assistance.

Alexander, Lyn. *The Doll Dressmaker's Guide to Pattern Making*. Available from Hobby House Press.

Alexander, Lyn. *The Doll's Shoemaker*. Available from Hobby House Press.

Back, Pieter. *Textile, Costume and Doll Collections in the U.S. and Canada*. Available from Hobby House Press.

Bailey, Albina. *19th Century Bonnets and Hats for Dolls*. Available from Hobby House Press.

Left: Cindy McClure's fairies. Creating is fun, but Cindy set goals for herself and reached them. Her success lies in her ability to create quickly. See the "Dollionaire" story about Cindy on page 51.

Bailey, Albina. *19th Century Hairstyles—Hair Accessories*. Available from Hobby House Press.

Bailey, Albina. *How to Make 19th Century Shoes for Dolls*. Available from Hobby House Press.

"Basic Principles for the Care and Preservation of Period Costumes." National Museum of American History, Washington, D.C. Available at museums.

Boehm, Max. *Dolls*. New York: Dover, 1972.

Coleman, Dorothy, Elizabeth and Evelyn. *The Collector's Encyclopedia of Dolls*. New York: Crown Publishers, 1968.

David, Jay. *How to Play the Moonlighting Game*. Facts on File, Inc., 1983.

Davies, Nina S. *The Jumeau Doll Story*. Washington, D.C.: Hobby House, 1957.

Doll Patterns. Reprints from 1881. Available from Hobby House Press.

Durand, Diane. *The Art of English Smocking*. Available from Hobby House Press.

Ein, Claudia. *How to Design Your Own Clothes and Make Your Own Patterns*. Available from Hobby House Press.

Fikioris, Margaret A. "Textile Cleaning and Storage." *Museum News*, Vol. 55, No. 1, Sept-Oct., 1976. Available from museums.

Foulke, Jan. *Dolls and Values, Blue Book*. (any edition) Cumberland, MD: Hobby House Press.

Foulke, Jan. *Kestner—King of Dollmakers*. Cumberland, MD: Hobby House Press, 1980.

French Fashion Plates from the Gazette, Du Bonton, LePapé 1912 to 1925. Available from Hobby House Press.

Goldstein, Gerome. *Sideline Business, a Newsletter for Moonlighters*.

Guldbeck, L. *The Care of Historical Collections*. Associates for State and Local History. Available at museums.

Hat Making for Dolls 1855-1916. Reprints available from Hobby House Press.

"How to Wet-Clean Undyed Cotton and Linen." Information Leaflet No. 478, Smithsonian Institution Museum of History and Technology, 1967. Available from museums.

Jendrick, Barbara. *Doll's Dressmaker 1896*. Reprints available from Hobby House Press.

Johnson, Barbara. *Private Consulting*. New York: Prentice Hall.

Kämmer and Reinhardt Catalog of Dolls, reprinted by Doll Research Projects. Available from Hobby House Press.

Kamoroff, Bernard, C.P.A. *Small Time Operator: How to Start Your Own Small Business, Keep Your Books, Pay Your Taxes & Stay Out of Trouble*. Order direct: Bell Springs Publishing Co., P.O. Box 640, Laytonville, CA.

Kelley, Robert. *Consulting, a Complete Guide to a Profitable Career*. New York: Scribners.

King, Constance Eileen. *Jumeau*. Cumberland, Md.: Hobby House Press, 1983.

King, Constance Eileen. *The Collector's History of Dolls*. New York: St. Martins, 1977.

Klein, N. *Repairing and Restoring China and Glass: The Klein Method.* Order direct: P.O. Box 245, Harleyville, PA 19438

Lant, Jeffrey. *Consultant's Kit, Unabashed Self-Promote Guide.* Order direct: 50 Follen St., Suite 507, Cambridge, MA 01138.

J.K. Lasser Tax Institutes. *How to Run a Small Business.* New York: McGraw Hill.

Long, Ida and Ernest, *A Catalog of Dolls, 1877-1961.* Order direct: P.O.Box 272, Mokelumne Hill, CA 95245.

Mancuso, Joseph R. *How to Start, Finance and Manage Your Own Small Business.* New York: Prentice Hall.

Mancuso, Joseph R. *Sources of Help for Entrepreneurs.* New York: Prentice Hall.

Morgan, Mary. *How to Dress an Old Fashioned Doll.* Available from Hobby House Press.

1914 Marshall Field's & Co. Catalog, reprinted by Hobby House Press.

Noble, John. *Treasury of Beautiful Dolls.* New York: Hawthorn Books, 1971.

"Procedures for Cleaning Cotton Textiles." Eleanor Touceda Workshop, No. 4, Sept. 1951. The Textile Museum, Washington, D.C. Available from museums.

Putnam, K.G. *Caring for Textiles.* New York, Watson-Guptill, 1977.

Ravi, Albert, Editor. *Dolls Values Quarterly,* Cumberland, MD: Hobby House Press.

Rennelt, Francis. *Collector's Book of Fashion.* New York, Crown Publishers, 1982.

Oriental Simon & Halbig doll on right wears original costume. Armand Marseille boy doll on left wears simple reproduction outfit of pants and top. Making reproduction costumes is always a good business if you're talented.

Sears, Roebuck Catalog. Reprints available from Hobby House Press.

Seeley, Mildred and Colleen. *Doll Collecting for Fun & Profit.* Tucson, AZ: HPBooks, 1982.

Seeley, Mildred and Colleen. *Doll Costuming.* Tucson, AZ: HPBooks, 1984.

Seeley, Mildred and Vernon. *How to Collect French Bébé Dolls.* Tucson, AZ: HPBooks, 1985.

Seeley, Mildred and Vernon. *How to Collect French Fashions Dolls.* Tucson, AZ: HPBooks, 1985.

Serkis, Susan. *The Wish Booklets*. West Point, NY, 1965.

St. George, Eleanor. *The Dolls of Yesterday*. New York: Scribner's, 1948.

Tarcher, Jeremy P. *Working From Home*. New York: Houghton Mifflin.

Taylor, Charlotte. *Entrepreneurial Workbook—Step-by-Step Guide to Operating Your Own Small Business*. New American Library.

The Writer's Handbook. Boston: The Writer, Inc., 120 Boylston St., Boston, MA 02116

The Young Ladies' Journal. Reprints available from Hobby House Press.

Ulseth, H. and Shannon, H. *Antique Children's Fashions*. Hobby House Press, 1982.

Victorian Costumes. Reprint from *Harper's Bazaar*, 1867 to 1898. Available from Hobby House Press.

Westfall, Marty. *The Handbook of Doll Repair and Restoration*. New York, Crown, 1979.

White, Gwen. *European and American Dolls*. New York: Crescent Books, 1966.

Whitton, Margaret. *The Jumeau Story*. New York: Dover, 1980.

Reprints of magazines, such as *Peterson's*, *Delineator*, *The Doll Dressmaker*, and *Mme. Demorest*, available from Hobby House Press.

Note: See page 124 for address of Hobby House Press.

SMALL BUSINESS ADMINISTRATION BOOKLETS AND PAMPHLETS

The following booklets and pamphlets are available from the Small Business Administration, Washington, D.C., 20416.

Advertising, Packaging, and Labeling
For businesses that prepare their own ads, this pamphlet includes federal regulations, suggestions for successful ads, packaging, labeling, and public and private regulatory institutions.
1984, Doc. 129. $2.25.

Checklist for Going into Business
A checklist of things to consider before starting a small business.
1983, SBA 516N. Free.

How to Get Started With a Small Business Computer
Helps you figure out your business needs, what a computer can do to help and how to select proper hardware and software to meet those needs.
1984, SBA 453N. $.50.

Starting and Managing a Small Business of Your Own.
Information about starting and running a business.

Women's Handbook
How the SBA can help a woman establish a business.
1983, SBA 518N. Free.

MATERIALS AND SUPPLIES

Below and on the following pages is a list of materials and suppliers. Hopefully this will help you locate various items you may need.

All The Trimmings
P.O. Box 15528
Atlanta, GA 30333
Organdy, dotted Swiss, batiste, nainsook, voile and other fabrics and trims

Barglebaugh, Helen
118 Old Sutter Ave.
Jamaica, NY 11420
Shoe buckles and eyelet kits for shoes

Betty's Fabrics
821 State St.
Santa Barbara, CA 98101
Fine dress fabric and silks

Nancy and Jim Blair
P.O. Box 102
Westland, MI 48185
(313) 595-3003
Mechanical bodies

Britex Fabrics
146 Geary St.
San Francisco, CA 94108
Fine cottons, nainsook, dimity and other fabrics

Brookstone Co.
127 Vose Farm Road
Peterborough, NH 03458
Tools, hemostats, magnifiers, pantographs

California Millinery Supply Co.
718 S. Hill
Los Angeles, CA
Hat supplies

Carriage House Antiques
2 Lincoln West
New Oxford, PA 17350
Lace, edgings, lawn, nainsook, voile, organdy

Tony Carrillo
23-109 44th Ave. W. #B
Mountainlake Terrace, WA
Miniature marionettes and mechanicals

Commemorative Imports
Donald Herschel
Box D
Bayport, MN 55003
Doll plates, including my new French Fashion Lady plate

Conair Corp.
Miniature curling iron, 3/8-inch curl, called Conair Mini Curls, Model CD14. Good for human hair and mohair

Conservation Resources International Inc.
111 North Royal St.
Alexandria, VA 22314
Museum supplies for preserving dolls

Create-a-Doll
146 E. Chubbuck Rd.
Chubbuck, ID 83202
(208) 238-0433
Cork for stuffing

Creative Silk
820 Oakdale Rd.
Atlanta, GA 30307
Dress fabrics

DeMeo Brothers Importers and Distributors
75 Fifth Ave.
New York, NY 10003
Hair supplies

Tynie Baby, made by Horsmann, wears crocheted costume. Fine, delicate design is appropriate for this small baby doll. Ruth Klein is the designer of this original outfit and has been successful in this kind of doll-business venture.

Doll Chapeaux
435114 E. 6th Ave.
Portland, OR 97281
Bonnet patterns

Doll Repair Parts Inc.
9918 Loraine Ave.
Cleveland, OH 44102
Doll shoes, elastic and other doll supplies

Doll-Tiques
7836 Gratio
Richmond, MI 48062
Smocking machine

Dolls by Dottie
2910 Centerville
Dallas, TX 75228
Wigs, shoes, shoe buttons, bodies and other supplies

Dollspart Supply Co., Inc.
5-15 49th Ave.
Long Island City, NY 11101
Doll stands, wigs, eyes, shoes and other supplies

Elizabeth Zimmerman Ltd.
Babcock, WI 54413
Fine knitting needles, lace needles—1-1/4mm, 1-1/2mm, 1-3/4mm

Elsie's Exquisiques
205 Elizabeth Drive
Berrien Springs, MI 49102
Fabric, buttons, lace, ribbon

Exotic Silk
393 Main St.
Los Altos, CA 94022
Silks

Frank's Silhouette Parisian
P.O. Box 5
Laverne, CA 91750
Dress patterns

Lewis Goldstein
Rt. 3, Box M75
Sherwood, OR 97140

Handcrafted by Dunstan
P.O. Box 9685
Denver, CO 80209
(303) 777-2054
Fine brown or white cabretta-leather bodies

Heirloom Patterns
Paule Fox
38936 Chicago Ave.
Wadsworth, IL 60083
Doll-dress patterns

Helmon Label Co.
5143 W. Diversey Ave.
Chicago, IL 60639
Makes labels of your design

Hobby House Press
900 Frederich St.
Cumberland, MD 21502
(301) 759-3770
Patterns and books

Home Silk Shop
2002 E. McDowell
Phoenix, AZ 85006
and
3305 S. Cienega Blvd.
Los Angeles, CA
Silks

Home-Sew Inc.
Bethlehem, PA 18018
Tiny buttons and lace

International Old Laces, Inc.
Martha Frey—Membership Chairman
4212 Bel Pre Rd.
Rockville, MD 20883
Lace making

Isbell Printing Co.
2535 N. Jack Rabbit Ave.
Tucson, AZ 85745
(602) 792-2791
Printer of World Doll Day logo

Muriel Kramer
1127 Lover Drive
Kent, OH 44240
Dolls for conventions

Laces
2982 Adeline St.
Berkeley, CA 94705
(415) 845-7178
Laces, lace-making equipment, tatting equipment, antique linen, silk pongee, silk crepe, Swiss batiste, silk crepelene, thread and needles

Lady K Fashions
P.O. Box 845
New Port, OR 97365
Doll-dress patterns

Lyn's Doll House
P.O. Box 8341
Denver, CO 80201
Doll-dress patterns, shoe patterns

MacDowell Doll Museum
Route 1, Box 15A
Aldie, VA 22001
Repairs bisque dolls

Manny's Millinery Supply
63 West 38th St.
New York, NY 10018
Hat supplies

Marty's House of Dolls
Rt. 4, Box 108
Carmi, IL 62821
(618) 382-2209
Repairs dolls

Mays Ceramics
15041 Leffingwell
Whittier, CA 90604
(213) 941-5375
Paperweight eyes

Meyer Jacoby & Sons Inc.
32 W. 20th St.
New York, NY 10011
Wigmaker

Mini-Magic Carpet
3675 Reed Rd.
Columbus, OH 43220
Patterned silk, straw hats, French lace

Naibert, Janice
16590 Emory Lane
Rockville, MO 20850
Fancy French trim, ribbon, buttons, some fabric

National Art Craft Co.
23456 Mercantile Rd.
Commerce Park
Beachwood, OH 44122
Lace, doll globes, craft supplies

O'Brien, Anne
11208 Tiara
North Hollywood, CA 91601
Millinery supplies, covered wire, feathers, silk flowers, straw hats

Reinhold Lesch
18633 Rodental
Coburger Strasse 47
Pasyach 17 West Germany
New glass eyes for dolls

Schoepher
138 W. 31st St.
New York, NY 10001
Old glass eyes

Smith, D.
2125 W. 19th Pl.
Eugene, OR 97405
Hats for dolls

Standard Doll Co.
2-83 31st St.
Long Island City, NY 11105
Tiny buttons of all sizes, doll supplies, doll stands

Stevens, Mary K.
121 E. Main St.
Roselle, IL 60172
Patterns and doll supplies

Terry's Leather Goods, Inc.
4965 S. Broadway
Denver, CO 80110
(303) 781-0121
Leather

The Doll Dresser
P.O. Box 10787
Glendale, CA 91209
Authentic patterns for doll dresses

Thimble House
R.D. 1, Box 406
Center Valley, PA 18034
Makes bonnets for French and German dolls

Treadleart
25834 Narbonne Ave.
Lomita, CA 90717
Thread, disappearing markers, sewing supplies

Ulseth, Hazel
4483 Grellick Rd.
Traverse City, MI 49684
Doll-dress patterns

Vivian Sloane
Viv's Ribbons and Lace
212 Virginia Hill Drive
Martinez, CA 94553
Laces, ribbon, decorations

Wemzel, May
38 Middlesex Dr.
St. Louis, MO 63144
Publishes Costume Quarterly

White, Lucy
P.O. Box 982
Westbrook, CT 06498
Mohair and lambskin for wigs

Yesterday's Patterns
P.O. Box 2053
Falls Church, VA 22042
French dress patterns

DEALER LIST

Below is a list of some dealers with whom we have dealt in the past. We have not intentionally left anyone off the list. Most dealers do business by telephone and will ship dolls with a 3-day-return privilege. Dealers also attend various doll shows; some dealers listed do business *only* at doll shows. Some dealers have doll lists, and some have display ads in doll magazines.

Cohen, Marcia
Cohen Auctions
P.O. Box 425—Rtes. 20-22
New Lebanon, NY 12125
(518) 794-7477
Most Cohen auctions contain some fine French fashion dolls.

Confederate Dollers
P.O. Box 24485
New Orleans, LA 70124
(504) 488-2967
Sells dolls at doll shows.

Fernando, Jim
370 Fair Oaks St.
San Francisco, CA 94110
(415) 282-9967
Sells dolls at doll shows; also dresses dolls.

Harten, Helen
Red Door Antiques
Prescott, AZ 86031
(602) 445-4691
Carries selection of French fashion dolls.

Haynes, Mickie
4238 N. 7th Ave.
Phoenix, AZ 85013
(602) 264-1186
Has doll furniture for props and dolls.

Kaner, Jackie
9420 Reseda Blvd.
Northridge, CA 91325
Sells dolls at doll shows.

Kimport Dolls
P.O. Box 495
Independence, MO 64051
(816) 833-0517
Sells dolls by mail order or at doll shows. Publishes Doll Talk.

Luzzi, Marlene
4 Fernwood Way
San Rafael, CA 94901
(415) 454-7164
Sells dolls by mail order or at doll shows.

Martin, Marshall and Don Christenson
45 Eucalyptus Knoll
Mill Valley, CA 94941
Sells dolls by mail order or at doll shows. Dresses some dolls.

McIntyre, Elizabeth
P.O. Box 105, RT 183
Colebrook, CT 06021
(203) 379-4726
Sells dolls by mail order or at doll shows.

Melton, Julia
P.O. Box 13311
Chesapeake, VA 23325
(804) 420-5117 or 420-9226
Sells dolls by mail order.

Joel Pearson and Joe Jackson
5879 Gen Haig
New Orlean, LA 70124

Ralph's Antique Dolls
7 Main St.
Parksville, MO 64152
(816) 741-3120 or 741-7699
Sells dolls at doll shows. Has doll shop and museum.

Richard Right Antiques
P.O. Box 187
Birchrunville, PA 19411
(215) 827-7442
Sells dolls by mail order, at doll shows and doll shop.

Robbins, Carolyn
Sells dolls at doll shows.

Rockwell, Karen
Sells dolls at doll shows.

Tyrrell, Billie Nelson
P.O. Box 1000
Studio City, CA 91604
Sells dolls at doll shows.

West, Ruth
1 N. Main St.
Parksville, MO 64152
(816) 741-5701
Sells dolls at doll shop and doll shows.

DOLL MUSEUMS

Below and on the following pages is a list of doll museums you may want to visit. These museums contain many different kinds of dolls. Some museums are only open part of the year, so before you visit, be sure to contact them to see what they display in the museum and when they're open.

Adirondack Center Museum
Court St.
Elizabethtown, NY 12932

Alfred P. Sloan Museum
1221 E. Kearsley St.
Flint, MI 48503

Angels Attic
516 Colorado Ave.
Santa Monica, CA 90401

Left: Snow Angel is a masterpiece by Jim Fernando, a present-day doll couturier. Doll is an A7T. Jim designed and made her fantastic costume—even her white-feather-and-eiderdown wings! Creating beautiful costumes is always a talent in demand.

Anita's Doll Museum &
Boutique
6737 Vesper Ave.
Van Nuys, CA 91405

Antique Doll Museum
1721 Broadway
Galveston, TX

Aunt Lens Doll & Toy
Museum
6 Hamilton Terrace
New York, NY 10031

Bazaar Cada Dia
2801 Leavenworth
San Francisco, CA 94133

Brooklyn Children's Museum
145 Brooklyn Ave.
Brooklyn, NY 11213

Cameron's Doll & Carriage
Museum
218 Becker's Lane
Manitou Springs, CO 80829

Camp McKensie Doll
Museum
Mudo, SD 57559

Children's Museum
3000 N. Meridian St.
Indianapolis, IN 46206

Children's Museum
300 Congress St.
Boston, MA 02210

Children's Museum
67 E. Kirbey
Detroit, MI 48202

Christine's Doll Museum
4940 E. Speedway
Tucson, AZ 85712

Cotonlandia Museum
P.O. Box 1635
Greenwood, MS 38930

Crafty Owl Shop & Doll
Museum
470 Washington Ave. N.
New Haven, CT 06512

Cupids Bow Doll Museum
958 Cambridge Ave.
Sunnyvale, CA 94087

Diminutive Doll Domain
Box 757
Indian Brook Rd.
Greene, NY 13778

Disney Dolls Museum
Grand Lake'O the Cherokees
Disney, OK 74340

Doll Cabinet & Museum
Star Rt., Box 221
Ferriday, LA 71334

Doll Castle Doll Museum
37 Belvedere Ave.
Washington, NJ 07882

Doll Museum & Trading Post
Highway 30
Legrand, IA 50142

Doll Museum at Anne Le
Ceglis
5000 Calley
Norfolk, VA 23508

Dolls Den & Museum
406 River Ave.
Point Pleasant Beach, NJ
08742

Dolls in Wonderland
9 King St.
St. Augustine, FL 32084

Dolly Wares Doll Museum
3620 101 North
Florence, OR 97439

1840 Doll House Museum
196 Whitfield
Guilford, CT 06437

Enchanted World Doll
Museum
Sioux Falls, SD

Essie's Doll Museum
Rt. 16, Beech Bend Rd.
Bowling Green, KY 42101

Fairbanks Doll Museum
Hall Rd. (off Rt. 131)
Sturbridge, MA

Fairhaven Doll Museum
384 Alden Rd.
Fairhaven, MA 02719

Gay 90's Button & Doll
Museum
Rt. 1, Box 78
Eureka Springs, AR 72632

Gerwecks Doll Museum
6299 Dixon Rd.
Monroe, MI 48161

Geuther's Doll Museum
188 N. Main St.
Eureka Springs, AR 72632

Ginny's Doll Shop and
Museum
1117 S. Florida Ave.
Lakeland, FL 33803

Good Fairy Doll Museum
205 Walnut Ave.
Cranford, NJ 07016

Greenfield Village & Museum
Oakwood Blvd.
Dearborn, MI 48121

Hawley Rose Museum
305 E. Filer St.
Ludington, MI 49431

Heirloom Doll
Hospital/Shop/Museum
416 E. Broadway
Waukesha, WI 53186

Helen Moe Antique Doll
Museum
Hwy. 101 and Wellsona Rd.
Paso Robles, CA 93446

Hennepin County Historical
Society
2303 Third Ave. South
Minneapolis, MN 55404

Hidden Magie Museum
4015 California
Norco, CA 91760

Hobby Horse Doll/Toy
Museum
5310 Junius
Dallas, TX 78214

Homosassa Doll Museum
Rt. 5, Box 145
Homosassa, FL 32646

Jacksonville Doll Museum
5th & California St.
Jacksonville, OR 97530

Jonaires Doll & Toy Museum
Rt. 4, Box 4476
Stroudsburg, PA 18360

Kentucky Museum
Western Kentucky University
Bowling Green, KY 42101

Klehms Pink Peony Doll
2 E. Algonquin Rd.
Arlington Heights, IL 60005

Knotts Berry Farm Miniature
Museum
8039 Beach Blvd.
Buena Park, CA 90261

Lolly's Doll & Toy Museum
225 Magazine St.
Galena, IL 61036

Madame Alexander's Doll
Museum
711 S. 3rd Ave.
Chatsworth, GA 30705

Magic Mountain Doll
Museum
Big Bear Lake, CA 92315

Margaret Woodbury Strong
1 Manhattan Square
Rochester, NY 14607

McCurdy Historical Doll
Museum
246 N. 100 East
Provo, UT 84601

Memory Lane Doll & Toy
Museum
Old Mystic Village
Mystic, CT 06355

Mary Merritt Doll Museum
Rt. 2
Douglassville, PA 19518

Milan Historical Museum
10 Edison Dr.
Milan, OH 44846

Museum of Antique Dolls
505 E. President St.
Savannah, GA 31401

Museum of Collectable Dolls
1117 S. Florida Ave.
Lakeland, FL 33803

Museum of Science &
Industry
57th Street
Chicaco, IL 60637

Neill Museum
P.O. Box 801
Fort Davis, TX 79734

Old Brown House Doll
Museum
1421 Ave. F
Gothenburg, NE 69138

Old Rectory
50 W. New England
Worthington, OH 43085

Playhouse Museum Old Dolls
& Toys
1201 N. 2nd St.
Las Cruces, NM 88005

Pioneer Museum
215 S. Tejon
Colorado Springs, CO 80903

Poor Doll's Shop Museum
RR 2, Box 58
Syracuse, IN 46567

Portland Museum of Art
7 Congress Square
Portland, ME 04101

Santa Barbara Museum of Art
1130 State St.
Santa Barbara, CA 93101

Society of Memories Doll
Museum
813 N. 2nd St.
St. Joseph, MO 64502

Space Farms Zoo & Museum
RFD 6, Box 135
Sussex, NJ 07460

Storybook Museum
620 Louis St.
Kerrville, TX 78028

Thomas County Museum
1525 W. 4th St.
Colby, KS 67701

Time Was Village Museum
Rt. 51 (4 miles south)
Mendota, IL 61342

Town of Yorktown Museum & Shop
1974 Commerce St.
Yorktown Heights, NY 10598

Toy Museum of Atlanta
2800 Peachtree Rd. N.E.
Atlanta, GA 30305

Treasure House Doll Museum
1215 W. Will Rogers
Claremore, OK 74017

University Historical Museum
Illinois State University
Normal, IL 61761

Victorian Doll Museum
4332 Buffalo Rd., Rt. 33
Rochester, NY 14514

Washington Dolls' House Museum
5236 44th St. NW
Washington, DC 20015

Wenham Historical Museum
132 Main St.
Wenham, MA 01984

This reproduction costume for a K(star)R 101 was copied by Jackie Jones from a regional costume of another K(star)R 101. Reproducing regional costumes can be very profitable.

White House Doll & Toy Museum
1238 S. Beach Blvd.
Anaheim, CA 92804

Wilkinsons Museum
3076 Morningside Dr.
Salt Lake City, UT 84124

Yesteryears Doll Museum
Main & River Sts.
Sandwich, MA 02563

AUCTION HOUSES

Below is a list of auction houses that hold doll auctions around the country.

Auctions by Theriaults
P.O. Box 151
Annapolis, MD 21404
(301) 269-0681
Holds auctions about once a month. Has cataloged and uncataloged aucions in and around major cities; moves from place to place. Absentee bidding permitted.

Cohen Auctions
P.O. Box 425—Rtes. 20-22
New Lebanon, NY 12125
(518) 794-7477
Cohen auctions always contain some fine French and German dolls.

Kenneth S. Hays & Associates, Inc.
4740 Bardstown Rd.
Louisville, KY 40218
Holds doll auctions when he has a collection to sell. Watch doll magazines for times and places.

Richard W. Withington, Inc.
Hillsboro, NH 03244
(603) 464-3232
Holds cataloged auctions about once a month. No absentee bidding.

Other auction houses that sell dolls periodically are listed below and in the next column.

Richard A. Bourne Co., Inc.
P.O. Box 141
Hyannis Port, MA 02647

Christie's
912 E. 67th St.
New York, NY 10021

Dumouchelle Art Galleries Co.
409 E. Jefferson Ave.
Detroit, MI 48226

Sotheby Park Bernet
1334 York Ave. at 72nd St.
New York, NY 10021
and
7660 Beverly Blvd.
Los Angeles, CA 90036

VIDEOTAPES

Check out this list of videotapes. Most need to be ordered from the supplier. I have not viewed these tapes.

Basic Doll Making, $49.95.
Dolls by Dottie
2910 Centerville
Dallas, TX 75228

Composition Doll Repair, $49.95
Invisible Porcelain Repair, $99.95.
Dolls By Joyce
8985 Wayne Rd.
Westland, MI 48185

Doll-Making Techniques, $49.95.
Jewel Sommars
P.O. Box 62222
Sunnyvale, CA 94088
(408) 732-7177

Making Dolls, $49.95.
Janice Cuthbert
Seeley's Ceramics
9 River St.
Oneonta, NY 11382
(800) 847-2547

Making a French Reproduction Doll, $59.95
Making a German Reproduction Baby Doll, $59.95.
The History of Dolls and Their Evaluations, $59.95
Dolls by B. Frank
1042 Minnetonka Rd.
Severn, MD 21144

Sculpting and Mold Making, $49.95.
L. Brothers
3320 Crest
Farmington, MI 48024

OTHER NAMES AND ADDRESSES THAT MAY HELP YOU

Dana Rouse, Vice President for Programming, Denver Mountain Network.
(Markets and distributes programs for Public Broadcasting System—PBS)—Tapes and how-to-shows. There is a market for good how-to videotapes and programs on dolls.

Elderhostel
80 Boylston St., Suite 400
Boston, MA 02116
Elderhostel has programs all over the United States and in Europe for older people. Doll-making classes and doll-interest classes could be taught in any of these places.

National Home Business Report (bimonthly publication)
Barbara Brabee Productions
P.O. Box 2137
Naperville, IL 60566

Office of Small Business Development Centers
Small Business Administration
Washington, D.C. 20416

Southeastern Doll Symposium
Office of Continuing Education
Meridith College
Raleigh, NC 27611
(919) 833-6461

Right: Antique doll in original costume, marked *3H,* is rare. She has universal appeal and will gradually increase in value.

Comprehensive Glossary

As with the information in the previous section, I want to provide you with tools—this section includes definitions of some of the terms you might encounter in your daily life in the doll world. Hopefully this information can be used by knowledgeable doll people *and* those who are just beginning. Defining some of the more common terms will allow a person just entering the doll world to know what people are talking about. And even if you've been around for a long time, there may be some things you want to look up.

A.M.—Initials found on bisque dolls made by Armand Marseille, a German doll maker, from about 1895 to 1925.

A.T.—Dolls, probably made by A. Thuillier, that had leather bodies or jointed, composition bodies.

Absentee bid—Bidding at auction, either by mail or phone, without being there in person.

Adams, Emma—Maker of rag dolls. She painted features and hair on every doll she made until her death in 1900.

Advertising dolls—Doll made to advertise or promote a product, such as Campbell's Soup kids or Morton's Salt girl.

All-bisque—Term used when entire doll is made of bisque.

Angora—Soft hair from goat used for early doll wigs.

Antique dolls—Dolls over 75 years old.

Applied ears—Ears made separately from the head and attached after head is removed from mold. Found in older French dolls.

Articulation—When used with dolls, refers to the jointing of doll for possible movement.

Baby Bo Kaye—Boy baby doll with celluloid or bisque head, composition limbs, cloth body, voice box and molded hair. Copyrighted in 1926.

Left: Hazel Samuelson specializes in costuming doll-house dolls. Here is a spectacular group of her 4- to 5-inch reproduction dolls.

Bald heads—Dome-shaped heads without hair.
Ball-jointed—Type of doll joint using a wood ball in the socket for flexibility in movement.
Ball-joints—Round wood bead used in joint to facilitate movement.
Bébé—Doll made to represent French child.
Belton—Early partner of Jumeau; no connection to bald-headed dolls has been found.
Belton-type—Bisque head made with two or more holes in the top, possibly to fasten a wig. Head is sometimes flattened but not cut open.
Bent-limb—Baby-type body in sitting position.
Bergoine—Name found on some Steiner dolls.
Biedermeier—China dolls with black spot painted on top of bald head.
Biskoline—Type of dull celluloid.
Bisque—Form of porcelain clay, fired or baked until it has chemically changed or melted. It is like the material of a fine dish, only without a glaze or shine. See *china head*.
Black light—Type of bulb used with dolls to see repairs through bisque. Other uses include to show minerals or to attract insects.
Blown eyes—Round glass eyes with stem where blow pipe was broken off. Eye looks like tiny Christmas ball. Used mainly in German dolls and dolls with sleep eyes.
Blush—Rosy color applied as cheek color or over eyes as shadow.
Bonnie Babe—Name of baby dolls made by Georgene Averill.
Breveté—French word for *patented*. *Bte* is abbreviated form used on some dolls.
Brownies—Cloth dolls based on the figures of Palmer Cox. Twelve different dolls appeared on 1 yard of cloth. Each doll had a front and back, which were cut out, then sewn together and stuffed.
Bru—French doll-making company.
Bye-Lo Baby—Baby doll designed and copyrighted by Grace Storey Putnam. Doll was fashioned after 3-day-old baby and was first made in wax. Body was made of cloth and stuffed.
Cabinet-size doll—Doll under 16 inches high.
Candy-store dolls—Small, inexpensive, all-bisque dolls, originally sold in candy stores.
Carriage trade—Wealthy people who purchased expensive dolls, such as those made by Jumeau and Bru, for their children.
Carton-pate—Pasteboard.
Cat's tongue—Type of brush used for painting mouths on dolls.
Celluloid—Originally was trade name for dolls made by the Hyatt Brothers. Dolls were made of a synthetic material composed of cellulose nitrate, camphor, pigments, fillers and alcohol.
Ceramic—Any fired clay product.
Character dolls—Lifelike representations of real people, especially children and babies. Dolls with realistic expressions.
Chemise—Plain dress that doll wore when it was sold; undergarment covering top part of body.
China clay—Fine white clay.
China head—Glazed porcelain shoulder heads with a shiny surface. Unglazed ceramic is *bisque* and glazed ceramic is *china*.
China mop—Large round brush with soft bristles used to apply face blush on dolls.
Closed mouth—Doll with lips modeled together.
Collectable dolls—Dolls between 25 and 75 years old.
Color rubs—Places where cheek color has been rubbed off.
Composition—Material (paper pulp, glue, wood chips, sawdust or grain) used to make doll bodies. Harder than papier-mâché.
Cone—Commercially made pyramid of clay that melts at exact temperature. Used for testing kiln temperatures.
Contemporary clothes—Clothing made about the time of the doll, but not necessarily the doll's original clothing.
Cork—Substance used for pates of many French dolls.
Crèche figures—Figures used in religious scenes that are sometimes collected as dolls.
Croquill pen—Art pen used today to paint lashes on reproduction dolls.
Crown—Open-crown or closed-crown refers to bisque over the top of the head. This was usually cut off to set in glass eyes. *Belton-type* is

the term often used for closed crowns.

Cuvets—Cuplike wood pieces inserted in legs and arms to make joints work better. Also used as reinforcement.

D.E.P.—Intials mean *registered*. *Déposé* in French; *deponier* in German.

D.R.G.M.—Registered design that stands for *Deutsches Reichs Gegraughs Muster.*

Déposé—Mark on doll's head that means *registered*.

Doll's markings—Doll's birthmark or company identification letters, size and mold numbers.

Dolly Dingle—Doll designed by Grace Drayton.

Double-jointed—Another term for ball-jointed.

F.G.—Initials found on some dolls made by François Gaultier, a French doll-head maker.

Fabricant—Manufacturer of dolls.

Feathering—Fine lines of eyebrow.

Fire—Heat clay to vitrification.

Flange necks—Type of neck usually found on baby dolls. A roll or flange on the neck widens to hold head in cloth body.

Flirty eyes—Eyes that move from side to side.

Flux—Glasslike substance that makes colors flow when melted with heat. Also makes colors glossy.

French fashion dolls—French lady dolls of the middle-to-late 19th century that were dressed in beautiful costumes.

Frozen Charlotte—Unjointed doll of bisque or china; some had molded hair, bonnets or wigs.

Fulper—American company. Fulper Pottery made bisque heads and some all-bisque dolls. Some heads had molded hair and painted eyes.

Gaultier, François—French doll-head maker.

Gazette—Porcelain screen or rack. Wafer of unfired porcelain is placed on screen or rack, along with greenware heads, for firing.

Gesland body—Knit-covered, stuffed doll bodies with metal armatures, or composition doll bodies.

Gladdie—Doll designed by Trobridge.

Glaze—Smooth, glossy, glasslike finish on porcelain.

Googly eyes—Eyes with pupil set or painted to the side.

Greenware—Unfired porcelain shape made by pouring slip into mold.

Gusset—Piece of leather or cloth inserted in joint of cloth or leather body to make joint movable.

Gutsell—Cloth boy doll.

Hairline crack—Tiny crack in bisque.

Hand-sculptured—Modeled by hand from a lump of clay.

Heubach—German maker of character dolls.

High cheek color—Lots of pink blush was added to cheeks.

Hundles—Flat, woven baskets that doll heads were dried in.

Huret—French doll maker.

Hydrocal—Very hard plaster used to make master molds.

Incassable—Unbreakable.

Incised—Indented into, as numbers pressed into unfired bisque.

Intaglio eyes—Painted eyes with pupil incised or indented.

Iris—Colored part of eye.

Jne—Jeune, Junior.

Jumeau—French doll-making company. Various Jumeau marks include: déposé (registered); E.J. (Emile Jumeau); incised déposé (word déposé is indented): Long-Faced (modeling of face is long on these early Jumeaus).

K(star)R—Doll-making company of Kämmer & Reinhardt. A star symbol is used between the initials K and R on the label.

Kaolin—Pure-white clay used for making dolls.

Kaolin vats—Large wood tubs in which clay was left to soak in preparation for making doll heads.

Kestner—Doll-making company.

Kewpie—Dolls designed by Rose O'Neill that had a unique appearance. Doll represented a fat child without clothes, with molded short hair. Kewpies were made of various materials, in many sizes. Some represented various occupations.

Kidiline—Inexpensive substitute for leather in doll bodies.

Kiln—Furnace designed to heat clay objects to vitrification. Wood was used to heat most old doll kilns, but modern kilns are electric.

Kissing doll—Right arm and hand raise to touch lips and throw a kiss. Put into action by pulling string.
Lady dolls—Dolls with an adult-female figure.
Laughing Baby—One of Georgene Averill's baby dolls.
Lignite—Decayed vegetation, often found in prepared porcelain slips.
Markings—Doll's identification letters or symbols usually incised or stamped on the back of doll's neck or head.
Marque, Albert—Sculptor who made dolls with bisque heads and composition bodies. Faces of Marque dolls are alike because he used only one mold. Marque dolls are *very* rare.
Marseille, Armand—German doll maker.
Mason-Taylor—Makers of Springfield wood dolls.
Master mold—Mold used to produce other molds. Originally made of hydrocal but now made of rubber.
Mechanicals—Dolls that perform in some way. Actions are activated by an enclosed mechanism. Many feature music boxes.
Mildew—Dark spots that appear on finished ware, usually caused when porcelain is underfired.
Milettes—Small French dolls under 14 inches tall.
Milliner's models—Dolls with papier-mâché heads and wood limbs that don't move.
Milvex—Type of colored composition developed by me and Vernon for making reproduction doll bodies.
Miniatures (minis)—Dolls under 5 inches high.
Mint—Original condition, not restored.
Mohair—Goat hair used for doll wigs. Hair is not as luxurious as angora.
Molded clothing—Clothing formed in the mold of the doll, not made of cloth.
Molded-hair toddlers—Toddler dolls with hair formed in the mold.
Motschmann—Doll bodies with porcelain sections joined together by leather or muslin. Steiner's Motschmann-type bodies are most well-known. He designed body after seeing Oriental dolls made that way.
Multifaced dolls—Head turns, exposing different expressions.
Name dolls—Dolls that have names incised on them by the manufacturer rather than names given by the owners.
Nodders—All-bisque dolls whose heads are loose but held on with elastic or other means so they move easily.
Open-closed mouth—Mouth modeled in open position but with no opening through the bisque.
Original—Artist's modeled doll or doll head used to make mold.
Original doll—This term is often misused. It usually refers to an original doll made of unfired clay. A mold is made of the doll and, in the process, the original doll is destroyed. True original dolls are those of carved wood, needlework and some rag dolls. It is a one-of-a-kind doll.
Oval eyes—Similar to paperweight eyes but *no* crystal added over pupil. Used mainly in antique lady dolls and some very early Steiner dolls.
Palette knife—Small, flat knife, similar to spreader, used by painters.
Paperweight eyes—Almond-shaped eye with bulge over eyeball of crystal that gives depth to the eye. Used mostly on French dolls.
Papier-mâché—Combination of paper pulp and glue used to make doll bodies, doll heads and other toys.
Parian—When used with dolls, it means a white porcelain. Collectors sometimes refer to untinted bisque dolls as *parian*.
Parisiènne—French fashion dolls.
Paste—Old term used for soft clay pressed in molds.

Left: Normandie-type bonnet is a reproduction made with antique materials. Hat making is always a talent that can be put to good use in the world of dolls.

Pate—Covering for an open head (crown). Usually cardboard in German dolls and cork in French dolls.
Penny woodens—Small, jointed, all-wood dolls with no fine details. They sold for pennies.
Plaster mold—Reverse form of doll made of plaster of Paris used to duplicate shape. Doll heads were produced by pouring molds with liquid clay.
Plaster pates—Pate made of plaster instead of cardboard or cork.
Pompadore—Red paint used to give rosiness to cheeks and lips. Used on antique and reproduction dolls.
Porcelain—High-fired, translucent, vitrified clays. May be unglazed, called *bisque*, glazed, called *china*, or white, unglazed with no overtinting, called *parian*.
Porcelain slip—Form of liquid clay made by adding water to porcelain. Slip is poured into molds. This replaced method of pressing paste clay in molds.
Portrait doll—Head modeled to resemble a person, often a celebrity.
Potassium silicate—Chemical added to wood chips to make doll hands hard and less breakable. Used by Jumeau.
Pounce—Wad of wool inside china-silk covering used to apply cheek color to porcelain dolls with a light, gentle up-and-down dabbing motion.
Printed dolls—Doll and clothing printed on yard goods to be cut and sewn, then stuffed by purchaser. Also called *cloth doll, rag doll* or *art-fabric-type doll*.
Pupil—Black center of doll eye.
Queen Anne—Type of wood doll.
Relief—Built up, as numbers on head raised above surface.
Reproduction—Exact copy, with identical painting.
Reproduction dolls—Dolls made by making a mold from an existing doll. Reproductions are always at least 16% smaller than the original doll.
Reproduction head—Head made from mold of an existing doll.
S.G.D.G.—Without government guarantee. Used with Breveté.
S.H.900s—Series of Simon & Halbig dolls with bald heads.
SFBJ—Stands for the *Société Française de Fabrication des Bébés et Jouets*. SFBJ was group of doll makers that made dolls after 1898. They collaborated to make dolls to sell at lower prices, and they produced the most common examples of French dolls.
Schmitt—French doll-making company.
Schoenhut—Doll-making firm that made wood dolls in Philadelphia from 1912 to the 1930s.
Scrubbie—Product with sponge on one side and rough, sandpaperlike substance on other side. Used to clean and polish bisque.
Shadow color—Color applied first to eyebrow section of doll. Feathering is added on top of color.
Shoulder head—Doll's head and shoulders are in one piece.
Shoulderplate—Top shoulder part of a doll, having an indentation for the neck to fit into.
Simon & Halbig—Doll-making firm.
Skippy—Composition doll designed to look like cartoon character, Skippy. Created by Percy L. Crosby.
Sleep eyes—Eyes with a closing mechanism.
Split head—Wax heads were slit open to insert hair, then closed.
Springfield dolls—Jointed wood dolls made in Vermont by Joel Ellis and Mason-Taylor.
Stamped—Markings stamped instead of incised.
Stamped doll—Doll with markings stamped on neck or body.
Steiner—Doll-making firm that made the Kicking Steiner, a mechanized doll that kicks, and the Walking Steiner, a mechanized doll that walks.
Straight wrists—Also called *gauntlet-type wrists* or *unjointed wrists*. Hand and forearm without joint.
Stringing—Putting jointed composition body together with elastic.

Swivel head—One-piece head and neck that turns in socket of shoulderplate.
Swivel neck—Head that turns in socket.
Synite—One ingredient of porcelain.
Terra cotta—Fired red clay.
Tête mark—Mark often found on Jumeaus dolls. *Tête Jumeau.*
Thuillier—A. Thuillier was a French doll maker.
Tuck comb—Small carved comb in the top of the hair. Used on some wood, jointed dolls.
Tynie Baby—Baby doll with bisque or composition head, soft body and voice box.
Unbroken wrists—Stiff wrists. Gauntlet-type wrists are unjointed composition. Hand and lower arm are one-piece.
Undercuts—Indentations that keep mold from pulling off clay model.
Vitrification—Bringing clay to point of chemical change from where it can never be returned to clay.
Voice box—Any mechanism installed in doll for making sounds.
Warp—To become misshapened in firing process.
Wax-over—To recoat with wax.
Whiteware—Old term for fired porcelain or bisque.
Wig—Hair arrangement on doll.
Wire-eyed—Eyes that open and close by use of lever behind ear or with controls in back of head. Steiner dolls with wire-eyed mechanism are most well-known.
Worn body—Doll that was played with until paint was partly worn off.
Yeux fibres—Eyes with white rays radiating from the pupil.

Prize-winning reproduction doll and dress are by Jill Gray, of Upwey, Victoria, Australia. Gray's skill as a designer and seamstress are always in demand.

Index